ELEVEN DOLLARS AND A HALF TANK OF GAS

ELEVEN DOLLARS AND A HALF TANK OF GAS

GREG DROST

BELLE ISLE BOOKS
www.belleislebooks.com

ISBN: 978-1-947860-50-6
LCCN: 2019939610

Designed by Michael Hardison
Production management by Haley Simpkiss

Printed in the United States of America

Published by Belle Isle Books (an imprint of Brandylane Publishers, Inc.)
5 S. 1st Street
Richmond, Virginia 23219

BELLE ISLE BOOKS
www.belleislebooks.com

belleislebooks.com | brandylanepublishers.com

For my wife and boys.

I blinked and suddenly I was forty, staring out the dingy windshield of my Honda Accord at a group of boys taking Sunday evening batting practice at the local ball field. It's a week until payday, but I just splurged on cheap coffee from the gas station. How did I get to this point in my life? How does anyone? Staring at the receipt, I am snapped back into reality by the metal ping of a bat from across the street. One of the boys roped a soft liner to left, arms raised in a brief moment of celebration. I take a long pull from my coffee as my head falls back against the headrest. I can sense the ghosts of long-departed memories drifting by in the afternoon light, echoing like the hallway of an empty school hours after the last bell.

I have eleven dollars in my bank account and half a tank of gas. Between the challenges of raising two boys and the endless grind of a demanding profession, I, like most, can feel myself being gradually run down both mentally and physically. There are times lately where my hands and legs will tremble for no reason that I can name. Life blows by so quickly, and as time ages our bodies, our decisions and experiences age our spirits. It's so easy to become feeble. The coach just delivered a meatball offering to a young lad, who smashed the pitch back through the middle of the infield. I chuckle to myself as the coach ducks emphatically to avoid decapitation.

It took me four decades to realize that time waits for no one. Sometimes we just have to make the best choices we can with what's in front of us, whether they turn out to be right or wrong in the end. I find myself briefly distracted by the center fielder as he tracks down the ball and lobs it effortlessly back toward the infield. I remember when life was as simple as the worry I felt after playing a night on the diamond. Solitary walks home in the summer twilight, taking in the sights, sounds, and thoughts of that exact moment, simply because it was where I was supposed to be. Unconsciously I reach down, half expecting to touch the grimy dust of the ball field encrusted in my jersey, to see the sweat stain on the inside brim of my ball cap, only to find my empty coffee cup. The world wasn't always simple then, but in those moments, I could swear it made a hell of a lot more sense.

PISS N BOOTS

At a very early age, I acquired an eccentric taste for cowboy boots. How exactly this fashion statement came about I can only speculate, although if I were to render a guess, I would say it had something to do with the Lone Ranger. However, where the Ranger sported his trademark black boots, I insisted on brown. I do vividly remember that I was quite particular about my boots; chalk it up to self-expression. This, I am certain, caused numerous issues for my parents, especially when they eventually had to send me out into the world. Preschool was my first opportunity to engage in social relationships outside of the walls of my family's home, and my social skills at that age were not top shelf. Looking back, the addition of the cowboy boots may have scared away a few potential playmates.

My preschool building was an archetypal schoolhouse, sporting faded chocolate oak board framing atop bronze-cider brick. A rustic bell hung high in an exterior alcove, below the peak of the A-frame roof. The lawn surrounding the building featured a number of weather-worn picnic tables, which were used for outdoor activities. The inside was dominated by a single enormous room, organized into a variety of play stations. There was the kitchen area, the large rug for circle time, a wooden rowboat on rockers that gave an authentic feeling of the rise and fall of waves, and a mammoth slide that required one to maneuver through a vast open-ended tube in order to cascade down a three-foot drop.

If the purpose of preschool is to foster the early development of social skills, then I have to say that it failed pretty miserably in my case. I often found myself playing in isolation along the outskirts of my preschool kingdom, immersed in a perilous gunfight with imaginary Indians, who were attempting to overtake me and kidnap my damsel—often played by a Barbie doll that I borrowed from the home living station. Most of my days were spent lost in the world of my imagination, and every activity designed to draw me out was misery. Circle time and show-and-tell were my personal purgatory. Being forced to contort myself to sit "Indian Style"—a skill I still have yet to master at the age of forty—and listen to Susie introduce her doll or Jimmy prattle on about his pocket jack set was about the most boring use of my time that I could think of. However, amidst the monotony of my preschool days, I did manage to secure my first ever arch nemesis. At the outset of this endeavor to record my memories, I took a solemn vow to respect the privacy of those who played a part in them, be it for good or ill. Thus, I shall refer to him as Phil.

Phil, to put it mildly, had an evil streak. He never hesitated to make my life a preschool hell, and of course he had the teachers fully duped. Phil worked tirelessly to stay in the good graces of the staff. He used impeccable manners when the teachers were present and was always quick to offer his assistance whenever necessary. In their eyes, he was the angel of the class, but I knew the truth behind his wicked ways. Whatever the reason, Phil targeted me from the start. He was quick on the draw with a negative comment, usually about my cowboy boots, and would do his best to discourage our fellow classmates from engaging in any form of play activities with me.

I don't know who came up with the saying that "sticks and stone could break your bones, but names can never hurt you," but it's a lie. Once, when I was in high school, I was jumped by a few fellas who had it in for my friend as we were practicing baseball together at the local park. I ended up with a swollen and distorted face, a few stitches to my upper lip, and several chipped teeth that I still sport to this day. Those wounds healed in a relatively short timeframe compared to some of the verbal jabs that I endured from Phil. I was a preschool cowboy, but I was no sheriff. Due to the nature of the situation, I was in no position to declare martial law upon my tormenter, and so chose the avenue of avoidance. But there was one day when my arch nemesis was able to get the best of me; a day that haunted me well past adolescence and into adulthood.

One of my most glaring physical weaknesses is that I have an extremely small bladder. I have missed crucial moments in movies and extended road trips by hours. When I finally received my driver's license, I took to keeping a plastic gallon jug in the back seat of my truck to ensure that an unexpected traffic jam didn't result in a ruined upholstery. The many misadventures caused by my bladder could fill a book of their own.

My preschool had a lousy bathroom situation. A set of faded white double saloon doors that hung on squeaky hinges led to two single-stall bathrooms—one for each gender. On the day in question, having been, as usual, in my own tiny world up until the bell sounded for circle time, I realized too late that I was in need of the facilities. I made a beeline for the swinging saloon doors, hoping to reach them before the class could fully organize themselves, but was wrangled by a passing teacher before I could make it. I found myself seated on a slight angle, almost directly across the carpet from Phil. Instantly, I knew he had observed the anxious discomfort on my face. Once everyone was seated, I took it as my opportunity and made a break once again for the bathroom. But Phil was sitting closer than I was, and he had me in his crosshairs. The second I got to my feet, he popped up and made for the double doors. I broke into a full-on gallop, but it was no use. I had just enough time to see him stick his tongue out before he slammed the door in my face. I knew exactly what was going to follow in short succession: Phil was going to take his sweet rosy time in there pretending to be hard at work, and I was going to be stuck out on the rug. Waiting. I thought for a brief moment about using the girl's bathroom instead, but fear of the unknown behind that forbidden door had me in knots. No matter that they were single-stall, boys were not allowed to use the girl's bathroom, end of discussion.

A teacher, having spotted our dash toward the bathroom, sent me back to the circle with a bladder full of urine, whereupon I was made to sit Indian style and wait patiently for my turn.

While adjusting my legs into the unnatural contortion, I knew it was only a matter of time before the inevitable happened. To make matters worse, we were seated in a boy-girl format, so to my immediate left and right sat two potential future wives that I was now going to destroy any hopes with. I sat and contemplated life as time ticked to a crawl, trying with all my might to focus on Johnny's presentation of his space shuttle—complete with two authentically dressed astronauts. I nodded along to every detail with excessive exaggeration until that moment of extreme euphoria hit and a high pitched shrill pierced the air. Instantly, my bubble of relief was replaced with a warm puddle of urine, to the dissatisfaction of my immediate neighbors. The shrill sound that filled the air caught on and was followed by more high-pitched screams and looks of horror from my classmates. The only upside was that, by the time the teachers regained control of the class, show-and-tell was ruined for everyone. I couldn't see him of course, but I can only assume that Phil was still sitting upon the porcelain throne with a sinister grin on his face. I was whisked away to one of the back rooms, where children were normally not taken except in drastic emergencies. There, I was made to change into a mismatched outfit that made my boots look utterly ridiculous: a pair of knee length yellow jam shorts accented with purple palm trees. Not necessarily a poor choice in complementary colors, but when combined with my green-and-red striped shirt, not a fantastic look on anyone. Also, the spare underwear they provided me with were extremely tight in the waistband. To top it all off, I remember the arrival of my mother and the exchange of the plastic bag containing my soiled garments. It was like a handoff of nuclear waste.

Really though, all you need to know about my preschool days, you could get from a glance at the outdoor class photograph. I was dressed in my finest button down, cords, and my cowboy boots. The photographer had the entire class lined up to the left of a giant tree and had a blue plastic chair reserved on the other side of the tree all for me. There I sat with a massive grin on my face, as my isolation was forever cemented into preschool history.

Needless to say, I was relieved to be heading into the real world of elementary school. I knew that life was going to instantly become better, because how could it get any worse? At the very least I was escaping from the presence of Phil and my legacy as the class sprinkler.

THE GREAT WHITE SHARK

My parents had opted to send my brothers and me to Catholic school, in hopes of giving us an education which would prove both academically and spiritually enlightening and might, in turn, provide guidance down any number of life's avenues. As I stood staring up at the two-story brick façade, awaiting my first day of kindergarten, all I could do was pray that the shoelaces my father had double-knotted for me the night before wouldn't come undone. I was fortunate that I only had to attend half-day kindergarten, because I knew that I was personally not ready for an entire day of intense learning. So there I stood, in my pressed khakis and white polo with matching socks, ready to take on the world. I watched as the morning class filtered out of the large metal doors and into the open arms of their ecstatic parents. My mind raced as I attempted to cling to my mother's leg, worried that I might not survive to flee through those doors to my own freedom that afternoon. In the back of my mind, I was still reeling from the difficulties I had endured during my time in preschool. But I was hopeful this experience would prove to be more favorable.

Suddenly, an elderly woman emerged from the building and introduced herself as Ms. McDonald, my teacher. I was immediately fascinated by her hair, silver and white in a way I had never known a person's hair could be. Completely transfixed, I floated through the heavy steel doors on the puffy white clouds of Ms. McDonald's hair. Thus, my academic career officially began.

Kindergarten presented me with the new challenge of

learning to color using all the colors in my crayon box and keeping inside the lines of the picture. I was quite comfortable with the color black, but it was now necessary for me to broaden my horizons. It took me a few weeks to get used to the new schedule, and the task of organizing my school supplies inside my desk, but eventually I began to feel as though I was getting the hang of it. But then Carrie walked into my life, and it all went sideways.

Carrie was tall and lanky and had the largest feet I had ever seen on a girl my age. I, by contrast, was the class runt: short and skinny, weighing in at a mere forty-five pounds. But as they say, love is blind, even if it is sometimes one-sided. Carrie was definitely eager for some runt pudding, and she let me know on a daily basis exactly what was on her mind. I was terrified, to put it mildly, and would fend off any and all advances with the ferocity of a caged lion. These sweet lips were mine, and I vowed to protect them at all costs.

I had learned early on that people are creatures of routine, and Carrie was no different. It was imperative that I always kept one step ahead of her in order to preserve my innocence. She was a crafty and cunning opponent, always lurking in the shadows for the opportunity to pounce on her sweet runt, smothering him with kindergarten love. It was no coincidence that I often found Carrie in line directly behind me, or standing next to me at the craft station. She had this amazing way of convincing my classmates that she needed to sit next to me on the carpet during circle time. I was not certain of Carrie's romantic intentions. Was she after a kiss? Or was it all nothing more than an elaborate game of pretend? Whatever her reasons, I quickly got into the habit of locating Carrie upon immediate entrance to our classroom and charting safe courses to keep optimal distance between her and my person. I adhered religiously to the theory of safety in numbers in order to deter any individual encounters that might end poorly on my part.

But distance could only save me from so much torment. Carrie taunted me from across the room with puckered lips and hand-blown kisses that made me shudder in my seat. Occasionally, I would find heart-shaped cards waiting for me in my cubby, with our initials over the acronym S.W.A.K.—Sealed with A Kiss. Whether through luck or vigilance, I was able to avoid any significant run-ins with Carrie for the better part of the school year. But sooner or later, every dog has his day.

The most fascinating part of our kindergarten classroom was a row of ancient floor-to-ceiling metal lockers. When pushed, the backs of the lockers would give way to approximately three feet of space before the back wall. Positioned on the back wall of the lockers were hooks and an elongated metal shelf that extended the entire length of the row. I would often venture into my locker to hang up my coat and book bag, only to resurface some twenty lockers to the left or right. Some students would frequently ask to go to their locker to retrieve an item from their book bag, and then refuse to come out at all. There was plenty of room for a kindergartener to maneuver through the maze of bags and coats. The same could not be said for an elderly woman trying to maintain order while chasing down a daydreamer lost in the lockers. I am sure it drove poor Ms. McDonald crazy to constantly have to go fishing for lost students in the middle of instructional time.

So it went one particular afternoon in late May, as I stood at my locker collecting my things and breathing a sigh of relief for surviving another half day of kindergarten, when a cold shadow fell across me. I felt her before I saw her, looming over my left shoulder, the way a seal probably feels a great white shark in the instant before the jaws of death close in.

With nowhere else to go, I shot like a bullet into the dark labyrinth of the coat room. I crashed through jackets and book bags, determined to outmaneuver the romantic vigilante on my tail. But Carrie, it seemed, had been thwarted in her overtures for long enough. Today was the day she would claim my lips as her trophy. I made a frantic dive for freedom out the adjacent locker, but smashed head-first into the back of the door. There was nowhere left to run. Carrie bore down on me like a hawk angling for a defenseless baby rabbit. Before I could wrap my head around the situation, Carrie's lips were pressed against mine. It was over in an instant. She vanished as suddenly as she'd appeared.

The final outcome had been resolved. Carrie never tried to kiss me again. I spent the rest of that year pondering the reason why as I continued to scribble furiously outside the lines of my coloring pages in thick black crayon. Was I a lousy kisser? Were my lips too chapped? Did I forget to brush my teeth? Or was Carrie solely interested in the chase, and now that it was over felt satisfied in her glorious triumph? I kept our moment of passion to myself for the remainder of the school year. My classmates appeared to be indifferent to the change in the dynamic between Carrie and me. To some degree, I was relieved that our romantic dance was over, but it haunted me on those sleepless summer nights. I never got an answer. Carrie moved away at the end of kindergarten.

BLUEBIRDS

The noise of Mrs. Q's small, polished, black-handled bell was one that I grew to despise over my first-grade year. It was a signal for our attention; but more than that, it meant the beginning of reading groups. As a teacher now myself, I must say that Mrs. Q had a marvelous setup for reading groups, complete with folding chairs, a throw carpet, and a blackboard to complement the lessons. The class was divided into three groups: Cardinals, Robins, and Bluebirds. I was initially delighted to be assigned to the Bluebirds at the start of the first quarter. Who wouldn't want to be a bluebird? The bluebird is exquisitely beautiful, if slightly territorial, and serves as a symbol of happiness and cheer in songs. I held my head high when Mrs. Q called the Bluebirds to the reading area and decorated my basal reader with the finest bluebird a young boy could draw.

It took me until to our second reading class together to realize that "Bluebirds" was code for "the slow kids." Mrs. Q attempted to disguise reading groups in a way that wouldn't draw attention to the variance in our reading abilities, calling the groups in a different order depending on the day, and shuffling the line-up card in hopes of not being too predictable, but six-year-olds are quite intelligent.

Reading, for me, was like the sound on an old tractor trying to turn over on an early fall morning. My tank had plenty of gas, my engine was in full choke, yet I couldn't get the ignition started. I tripped over sounds, blends, and words like an old drunk meandering down a poorly lit alley after last call. I knew every letter in the alphabet and its respective sound, so I was frustrated with my inability to put those letters together to form words. My fellow Bluebirds felt a similar plight, and we sought comfort with each other as we attempted to navigate through the treacherous reading waters. We stuttered, stammered, and sounded out the one-syllable words that the Robins and Cardinals breezed through. 'Read, damn it,' I told myself over and over again, patiently waiting for the day it would finally click.

While one reading group worked with Mrs. Q, the remaining students were expected to be working independently in our daily phonics workbook. My attention always strayed from the workbook, caught up in the sweet vocal tones of the Cardinals and Robins as they glided effortlessly through their books. I got caught up in fantasies of the day I would leave the Bluebirds and soar proudly with the Robins and Cardinals. On that day, I imagined, the class would erupt into a frenzied hysteria, hoisting me up on their shoulders while parading around the school for all to see. My fantasy popped like a bubble as Mrs. Q redirected me back to my workbook.

At night, I prayed to the Lord above to let me read tomorrow, wanting nothing more than the safety of my family and the ability to put words together. I didn't think I was asking for too much. Many of my peers were already quite successful, why should I be any different? I worked diligently in the same basal reader for an eternity. I slowly began to string the words together to form sentences. Maybe my progress was because I had been reading the same stories for over a month. Mrs. Q corrected me so often that I had begun to memorize the corrections, remembering the right words for all the wrong reasons.

As winter gave way to spring, my fellow Bluebirds and I continued to grind through basic words and simple sentences. Mrs. Q tried her best to conceal her frustration with persistent smiles and words of encouragement, but even when we finished a story, our fluency was so appalling that our comprehension was practically nil. I was never very successful at any story retells. The silver lining of life as a Bluebird was the alliance that we formed amongst ourselves. I was never going to stand by and let another student run off one of my Bluebirds. We stood together in the face of ridicule, especially when we were out of the safety of Mrs. Q's earshot.

Recess was the site of constant attacks on me and my fellow Bluebirds. Select Cardinals and Robins would corner us and mimic our choppy attempts at reading back in our faces. One lovely spring day, a few boys from class maneuvered Debbie, a Bluebird, into an isolated area just beyond the equipment shed in the back corner of the field. I happened to be nearby, and spotted Debbie as she was shrinking in on herself, obviously fighting back tears. I knew immediately what was going on. My suspicions were confirmed as I approached to provide backup and heard their malicious stammering teasing. After a few moments, I had heard enough. Seeing red, I threw all caution to the wind and charged into action with all the ferocity I could muster, uncorking a bloodcurdling war cry that echoed across the playground. I plowed head first into the instigator, knocking both of us squarely to the ground, and with catlike reflexes was back on my feet, towering over him like a prize fighter hovering over his opponent.

He lay there whimpering, staring up at me with trepidation in his eyes. I turned and delicately took the hand of my frightened comrade, attempting to soothe her pain.

My mind returning to present day, I recall that I need to help Emmett, my six-year old son, with his reading homework. Emmett is in first grade, and passionate about anything and everything I hold in high regard, but he struggles with reading the way I did at his age. It's hard to watch. All I can do is tell him every time, "We'll get there," and try to put the weight of experience behind my words.

RECONCILIATION

You never forget the first time you let one rip in mass. Now, I am not talking about some slight passage of air, smothered and muffled between creased khakis and a wooden pew that puts forth the weak sound of a dying duck. I am talking about a high powered, built up, festering explosion of gas that thunders off the rafters and echoes throughout the entire congregation. The type of heart-stopping fart that causes every head to whip around in search of the guilty party. A fart that warrants your best poker face for fear of the nun sitting at the end of your pew, which must be mirrored by those of the classmates in your immediate vicinity, regardless of the vulgar smell that accompanied it—an act of defiance that tapped into my inner Spartacus.

The church adjoining my elementary school was constructed of high-arching framed timbers, speckled and smattered with black knots. I spent many a school mass trying to count them, only to be interrupted by one of the nuns rendering an acute smack to the back of my skull.

The key to public flatulence in the house of the Almighty is to be extremely vigilant of the location of one's teacher, and to keep a sharp eye out for any lurking nuns in the immediate vicinity. The sisters were the ones to be mindful of, for their disciplinary practices were the stuff of legend amongst the lower grade levels. I had overheard the older students talking in the restrooms, and their tales were enough to leave me shuddering in horror behind the stall doors.

I often wondered if Father gathered the sisters in the back room for one final pep talk while the classes were traversing the corridor that united the school and church. It sure as hell looked like it. There stood the sisters, stoic and holier than ever. They broke rank like a well-oiled machine and spread out among the sinners to police for inappropriate mass protocol. When it was time to kneel, the sisters were watching to make sure one's rear end was not piggybacking on the edge of the pew. They watched carefully to ensure the students did not fidget with or deface their psalm books and listened with the same fervor to the amount of dedication put forth in times of song. Conversation of any kind during mass was snubbed out like a cigarette on the sole of a shoe. But few transgressions warranted more swift and terrible justice than breaking wind during the service, and to the unlucky soul that got caught, all that was left was to pray to the Lord for mercy. I remember seeing one boy yanked up by his earlobe and dragged down the main aisle and directly to the head sister's office. It was there that Sister would unleash the power of the wooden thunder, rendering a sore rump for a week.

In a few years of elementary school, I had managed to find myself in the head sister's office only once, and that was the result of pneumonia. I was so deathly ill that the nurse was

afraid to keep me in her office. Even in my weakened, delirious state I was still able to observe the heavy oak paddle leaning in the corner behind her desk, with a black leather grip and holes drilled across the striking surface—for aerodynamics, you see. The mere sight of the device sent a shiver to

After receiving my First Communion, this baby-blue suit and I were ready to take on the world.

my core as I was reminded of my many covert misdeeds during all-school mass. I never wanted to end up on the wrong end of that paddle.

As much as I hated school mass, even that couldn't hold a candle to the bane of every Catholic school childhood: the act of Reconciliation. Fortunately, I only had to participate a few times a year, but I remember the way it tied my stomach in knots. The prospect of Confession haunted me for days leading up to the booth, beginning the moment our teacher informed us that later in the week, the class would be confessing our sins to the Lord. My God, I was going to be forced to sit before a designated clergyman of the Almighty and confess the stupidity of my thoughts and actions. I began to imagine myself in that stifling confined space with an old, intimidating priest, sweat pouring down from my brow and back, praying that I would survive the interrogation. I often wondered if Father could read my thoughts; could tell that I was concealing some of my devious ways. Would I stutter and stammer as I confessed my wrongdoings, and flub my prayers beyond an acceptable point? When I left, would I feel cleansed of my sins, or tainted with guilt for being a lousy, prayer-forgetting child of the Lord?

The walk from the school to the church was always eerily silent when the day came, as individual clouds of sin permeated above us like haloes. Everyone was lost in deep reflection, silently rehearsing the confessional monologues that would bring them at least a glimmer of temporary salvation. The teachers and nuns would herd us into the last few pews and beckon us to pray while we waited for Father to absolve us of our sins.

My sins... Oh shit! To what degree was I going to allow Padre to enter into my disturbed and troubled mind? Was I to tell him all of my dirty thoughts, wrongdoings in the classroom, profanities I'd used on my brothers, or the fact that I was the culprit of many a disruptive mid-mass fart? Was an afterlife in Hell worth a few seconds of unpunished infamy amongst my peers? Well, probably not, so I would stick to the usual routine and just confess a few plausible-sounding minor sins, while keeping mum as to my more grievous misdeeds. No need to draw unnecessary attention to myself.

"Forgive me Father, for I have sinned. It has been several months since my last confession." My sins are: "I have said a few cuss words, been rude to my parents, and fought with my brothers."

"Is this all my son?"

"Yes Father."

And after stumbling through a few prayers with the assistance of the old padre, I was sent on my way to mutter a string of Hail-Marys to complete the absolution of my sins.

I was too young and conflicted to fully wrap my mind around the idea of living a life of restraint and obedience for the intangible rewards of eternal salvation in the afterlife. Already I found it cumbersome to reconcile my own thoughts on spirituality and moral goodness with that of the church. I was only seven years old and I was worried about how my thoughts and actions might permanently affect my overall purity as a person. I daresay it led to some weighty thoughts on my impressionable mind.

On the home front, my family was not especially religious. My parents expected us to say our nightly prayers, which I did before bed, asking the Lord to look out for my family and keep them safe. I vividly remember that I felt I had to mention each member of my family and extended family by name in order for the prayers to count. I never wanted to be mistaken for being too casual. At times, it was quite exhausting and time consuming while I rattled through every distant relative I could name.

I knew at the time that I believed in a power greater than myself, but I wasn't sure if I bought into all the regulations and rules that the church put forth. I think for me, finding faith was and continues to be a personal journey, so I try not to judge people for their beliefs. What works for one doesn't always work for the next person, and that is the beauty in choice. I never bought into weekly religious services and all-school masses because it wasn't the purest venue for me to express my thoughts and fears. But I think I needed those experiences to ultimately understand that for myself.

WHAT IS WRONG WITH ME?

Around the time that I entered the third grade, I went through a difficult period of self-awareness as I began to comprehend the true power the mind possesses over the body. The differences between myself and my peers were becoming more and more pronounced, and my classmates were beginning to take notice—as were the adults in my life. The changes manifested as if overnight, and they had a profound effect on my daily actions and interactions with others.

The first sign of my new dilemma was my inability to sit still in school. It was much more than just not being able to get comfortable in those old wooden school desks. Something that was rooted in my subconscious was directing my new affliction. I was in a freefall, and the more I struggled to gain control of my thoughts, the more I lost control of my actions. The worst part about it was that I had no idea what the hell was happening to me. Nor could I explain it to my parents or teacher.

I became an overnight medical phenomenon—at least to our family pediatrician's office. The physicians conducted a videotaped interview with my family on a Sunday morning when the practice was closed. They were fascinated with my behavior and asked my parents' consent to discuss my issue with other doctors. I think there was even discussion of putting my case in a medical journal. Ultimately, I couldn't have cared less about any technical medical diagnosis; I needed an answer that made sense to an eight-year-old.

"Why can't you keep still when you first sit down?" This was the question I was asked over and over again by doctors, parents, teachers, and eventually my peers—in the latter case mainly in the form of merciless ridicule that followed me well into sophomore year. What it boiled down to was that I couldn't sit still and focus until I had gone through a highly particular checklist that had imposed itself on my mind. I had to ensure that my shirt was precisely and tightly tucked into my trousers—absolutely no creases or wrinkles could be present. Next, it was imperative that my trousers felt comfortable against my skin, and against the surface I was sitting on. I would rock from side to side, tugging on the bottoms of my pants until I felt the desired level of comfort. Only then could I focus on the task at hand, but my systematic checklist needed to be fulfilled. To anyone watching, I'm sure it was nothing short of bizarre. God forbid I moved even a little from my seat after my checklist was satisfied, or else I would have to start all over again. Broken pencils, turning in papers, and being called to the board were a tribulation. When I reached middle school, changing classrooms became my personal hell. The sitting routine became an all-encompassing preoccupation. But how does someone in elementary school explain this to adults, and especially to peers? I couldn't. It's difficult to put it into words even now, thirty years later. So I did what any young person would do in an uncomfortable situation: I tried to hide it.

I was very open and upfront with my parents about how the sitting situation controlled and obsessed my thoughts. In elementary school it got to the point that my parents had to have a discussion with my teachers at the beginning of every year to explain the necessity of my routine. Both my teachers and parents were extremely supportive in trying to assist me with my dilemma. Now that I am a parent myself, reflecting back on that time I can only imagine the amount of daily stress that this caused my parents. As a parent and teacher, watching my own children and students struggle with personal hardships is a truly heart-wrenching experience for me. We try to offer suggestions, guidance, and advice, but there are some situations that are beyond our control. Unfortunately, there was no quick fix to this problem, and I know that was a difficult pill for my folks to swallow. I think what hurt them the most was the amount of ridicule that my peers lobbed in my direction over the next decade. It was innocent enough at first; stares that I could at least pretend to ignore while I squirmed in my chair as subtly as possible, seeking my optimal comfort level. The early years were filled more with questions and curiosity from my classmates than anything else. But curiosity soon gave way to insult, as I moved into my upper elementary and then middle school years. Things reached a head years later, when I transferred from Catholic school to a public middle school. I was able to conceal my problem in this new environment for a little over an hour, and soon had a small but dedicated band of unified bullies, themselves of fairly low social standing, whose only solace in life was evidently found in hurling hurtful comments my way when we passed in the halls, or else in drawing attention to my quirky behavior during class. I spent so much time on the defensive, desperately trying to keep my head down, that I could hardly focus on academics or friendships. I remember two things about eighth grade: I ate lunch with a small band of misfits, and I learned to walk with my head down. My doctors never could quite pin down what was causing my mind to run through this systematic checklist. It was suggested that it might be a form of Tourette syndrome, which my mother emphatically disagreed with. My own insight after years of reflection was that I was most likely suffering from some form of obsessive-compulsive disorder but was too young to make the connection. It was terribly difficult being teased for a problem of which I had no understanding. It took me until well into my high school years to gain control over my impulses, but I eventually got a better handle on it. In the long run, however, I think it has made me a more compassionate, empathetic, and patient individual than I otherwise might have been.

LOUIS AND THE ROMAN ARMY

The summer prior to my fourth-grade year, I had to have reconstructive surgery on my right knee. The initial damage had occurred while sliding into second base during a baseball game. The prognosis was a severe sprain, which condemned me to spend the next several months in a full leg immobilizer. Afterward, the doctors warned me to be careful and to take any strenuous activities slowly. So that was exactly what I was doing the day my mother sprayed me with the garden hose while I was walking back from the backyard swimming pool.

The frigid hose water came as a shock, and as I attempted to squirm away, I felt my right knee pop. My leg buckled instantly, and I crumpled to the concrete patio. It took my parents a few hours to realize that this was not a ploy for attention, but rather that something was drastically wrong. My worst fears were confirmed when the orthopedic specialist explained to my parents that I had a massive tear in my exterior meniscus, and surgery was going to be required. The surgery was put off for a week so that I could go on our family vacation to Virginia Beach. I love the beach, but not with one leg completely immobilized. I tried to make the best of it, and so did my family, but it was a difficult vacation nonetheless.

The last thing I remember prior to surgery was getting a shot in my rear end and lying on the operating table while the nurse told me to blow up a black balloon. After waking up, I puked into a bucket at the sight of the elevated cast that entombed my entire right leg. The remainder of the summer was nothing short of miserable. My leg itched uncontrollably in the heat and the cast made it impossible to scratch. My solution was to unwind a wire hanger and cram it down the opening at the top of my thigh. The crutches made my armpits ache with every step, and the rubbery smell of the useless foam pads was nauseating. While my brothers and friends spent the rest of the summer outside enjoying every freedom available to a boy of ten with no obligations, I was confined to the family room sofa to stew in my own misery. At this point in my life, I had yet to find my love of literature, so reading felt like a punishment, and our television got a grand total of five channels. I was so bored and lonely, I was actually excited when the start of the school year finally rolled around.

The status of my bum knee offered Ms. Walters, my teacher, a complicated dilemma when it came time for recess. On the one hand, I simply was not able to go outside due to the ratio of students to playground aides. However, our recess was the only period during the day when Ms. Walters could eat her lunch in peace. Eventually a compromise was reached: I was allowed to stay in the classroom during lunch and recess with another classmate for company. The solution certainly wasn't without its flaws, but it did allow me to rack up a few more fond lifelong memories.

Luckily, I had found comfort and companionship in a unique friendship that lasted well into high school. Louis and I had become friends toward the end of second grade—we just kind of fell into step one day. Louis and I were both on the outskirts of popularity in our class. Our classmates called Louis "Chicken Nugget," and it was not a term of endearment. He was a rather short and portly fellow, and he was teased quite a bit during our early elementary school years because of his weight. That said, he was unbelievably athletic for someone who had the build of a little dump truck. Baseball was a passion for the both of us, and we often got together on weekends to play ball at our elementary school field with Louis's older brother,

Edwardo. Those evenings, when I would shag the fly balls that rocketed off the end of Edwardo's bat as Louis threw batting practice under the setting sun, were some of the most memorable times of my childhood. When I returned to school that fall after surgery, there was never any doubt who I was going to ask to stay with me during lunch and recess. Louis graciously accepted, even though it meant he would be required to give up his outdoor recess every day.

Unfortunately, it must be said that Louis and I had a knack for getting into trouble whenever we spent time together. There was the infamous lemon meringue pie fight in the basement of his home: his sweet grandmother brought down a pie for Louis, Edwardo, and I to share after a family dinner one Saturday. Before she could even ascend to the top of the stairs, pie was flying everywhere. Too afraid to own up to our stupidity, we brought the pie plate upstairs and washed up for bed, only to be startled awake a few hours later by their father bellowing two floors below us. In high school, Louis drove a 1976 Ford Mustang with a siren alarm on it. It was his uncle's, and he'd given it to Louis for his sixteenth birthday. The best part about the siren alarm was that it had an on/off switch that sounded like a real police siren if you flipped it fast enough. We thought it was pretty amazing and went well with the five-dollar plastic police badges that we draped out the window when people pulled over as we cruised by. I knew, therefore, that the lack of adult supervision during these indoor lunch and recess periods would eventually prove disastrous. To this day, I still cannot for the life of me understand why Ms. Walters agreed to leave the two of us together unsupervised.

We had been back for several weeks, and it just so happened that the class was working on our first project of the year: a giant model of the solar system for science class. Ms. Walters had assigned students the responsibility of bringing in items of various sizes to represent the planets, which were now lined up neatly along the climate control unit under the window. There was a bouncy ball, a golf ball, a tennis ball, a soccer ball, a beach ball, and let us not forget Mother Earth herself, in the form of the class globe. Whether it was our curiosity that got the best of us, or boredom, Louis and I decided that we needed to conduct our own solar system research.

We tested the durability of Mercury by throwing it with all our might at the walls of the classroom, then diving for safety under the nearest desk as the planet ping ponged off the floors, ceilings, and walls. Baseball fans that we were, we thought nothing of having a game of catch with Mars, sending it whizzing back and forth across the length of the classroom. And if it occasionally went flying out the door and down the hall, well, who was around to see? Louis and I were both signed up to play soccer the following spring, so naturally we thought it was a grand idea to get some practice in with Jupiter for the upcoming season. Due to my limited mobility, I mostly contended myself with playing goalie in front of the lockers. Whenever Jupiter made it past me it made a horrific clanging racket, at least I didn't have to chase it down. (In the end, I only ended up playing one season of soccer; I played left fullback to Louis's right and I was terrible, mostly because I found no actual interest in the sport beyond the fact that our elderly Scottish coach was, my right hand to god, named Scotty.)

Within the space of a week, we had used every planet in the solar system except for the globe as a form of recreation. We never messed with Mother Earth. It was as if she held a revered sanctuary in our hearts—a sacred trust that lasted straight up until Tuesday's lunch period the following week, when we got bored again. Louis and I decided to take the globe apart from its stand to test the durability of our beloved planet. Louis's and my antics always started out innocent enough, but they could avalanche out of control in no time. Our first order of business was to test how well the earth rolled. We determined that this was best accomplished by rolling the planet down the main hallway of the fourth-and-fifth-grade wing. I positioned myself at one end, while Louis took the other. Initially we used hand power to propel the earth down the hallway, but this was shortly replaced by the use of our feet.

After several minutes of rolling the world back and forth down the hallway, Louis and I decided to observe how the earth might look while in orbit. We started in close proximity, tossing our planet with extreme sensitivity, only to take a step further with each successful toss. I felt like we were playing with a gigantic egg that would break open if we dropped it. We eventually ended up back in the classroom at opposite ends, hurling the earth into orbit with magnificent force. Louis had perfected the spinning technique of a disc thrower, if not the accuracy. We lost track of time as we pummeled our classroom globe. I reared back, sending Mother Earth sailing high into the air and right over the outstretched hands of my pudgy little friend. Together, we watched in horror as our planet soared directly out of the classroom window to plummet two stories down to the grassy field behind our school. At that moment, the damn recess bell rang.

In a full leg cast and crutches, there was no way I would be able to retrieve the globe before our teacher returned with the rest of the class. Our fate lay in the stumpy legs of Louis, who to his credit took off like a man shot from a canon. Time stood still as each second of the clock ticked by like the looming certainty of death itself. Louis and I had been in enough trouble that year already that another phone call home from Ms. Walters would surely spell the end of my existence. I stood in the doorway, gazing up and down the length of the hallway with shaking hands and ears ringing with a rising pitch like the speeding wings of approaching death. All I could do was pray that Godspeed Louis would make it back with the globe before the rest of the class arrived and try desperately to think up some excuse to use in the event that he didn't. None of my ideas rang true.

My heart stopped cold when, as if on cue, the unmistakable sound of many tramping footsteps coming up the stairs at the opposite end of the hall reached my ears, amplified by the concrete floors of the school to sound like the Roman army on the march. This was it.

My only solace was that I could play the injured soldier routine and hopefully gain myself some sympathy points. Poor Louis was up a creek without a paddle. The imminent sound of trudging sneakers grew louder and louder as the rest of the class made their way up to the fourth-grade hall. I cast one last look toward the back stairs, but only the blank hallway stared back. I was just about to give up and resign myself to facing Ms. Walters's wrath alone, when lo and behold! Louis appeared on the hall's horizon, globe in hand and sweating profusely.

It was Louis versus the Roman Army. Who would win this foot race? Louis reached the classroom just as the door to the second-floor hallway was creaking open. We had only enough time to place the globe—which had basically split in half at the equator—back in its rightful place and take our seats before the rest of the class entered the room. We did our best to look as innocent as possible; quite difficult considering Louis was dripping with sweat and huffing uneven breaths, to say nothing of the state of the planet.

At first not a single student, upon entering the classroom, appeared to notice that anything was out of the ordinary. It looked as if we had beaten the odds. For once, our lack of popularity may have worked in our favor. Until, of course, Ms. Walters entered the classroom and proclaimed that it was time for science class and we were going to spend the afternoon working on our solar system project. As the groups dispersed toward their designated planets, Louis's eyes caught mine—just as Sally cried out, over and over: "They destroyed Mother

Earth!" Ms. Walters took one look at the busted globe, then turned slowly with her hands firmly on her hips. In an instant, Louis and I knew our fate was sealed.

GINGER

The same year, I fell in love for the first time in my life. With the benefit of hindsight following my early experiences with Carrie, I was intrigued by the idea of love. Once in a blue moon, a girl would express some mild interest in me, but I tended not to reciprocate and they tended to move on after a few weeks. But all that changed when I met Ginger.

Ginger captivated my heart and mind with her otherworldly beauty and her skill on the kickball field. I was convinced that we were meant for each other. The only drawback was that she had no idea of the depths of my unrelenting love, and if she did, she did a very good job of hiding it. I was sure that I was barely a runty blip on her radar. Still, I obsessed over every brief interaction, every high-five on the kickball field, combing my memories second-by-second for any hint of flirtation.

Ginger had blonde hair that cascaded to the middle of her back, a smile that made my knees knock, and a pair of legs that made the school uniform worth wearing. The greatest gift Catholic school ever gave me was that wonderful dress code that served as my prepubescent introduction to the power of a woman's legs. Ginger didn't walk into a room, she floated, instantly commanding the attention of every boy in class. A slow, steady bead of sweat meandered down my spine every time I saw her, and I stammered through any attempt at meaningful conversation as if I had a mouth full of paste.

Daydreams, sweet daydreams filled my head and heart of running hand in hand with Ginger through a field of dandelions, or of afternoons filled with the sound of Ginger's laughter as I pushed her on the squeaky chain-link swings of the playground. Yet I knew our epic romance would never amount to the vision in my mind, because I could never work up the courage to ask her to be my girl. I daydreamed about it frequently, but what would a young woman of Ginger's stature ever find attractive in me? I had so little to offer, short, skinny, and knobby-kneed as I was.

Until, one vividly bright and fragrant day in late spring, Ms. Walters called a small group of students to her table to work in our basal readers. As fate would have it, Ginger slid into the seat next to mine. My heart instantly started to flutter, and I fought like hell to keep my nervous sweat to a minimum. It was impossible to concentrate on the task at hand with this demigoddess a mere inch or so from my unworthy self. Her beauty was an awe-inspiring force that drove my soul to the depths of grade-school depravity. I found myself caught up in fantasies of walking hand in hand with Ginger into the sunset of eternity, determined to enjoy this moment of close proximity for however long it lasted.

And suddenly, in an instant that changed my life forever, it happened. As we worked in our readers, Ginger shifted minutely in her seat, adjusted her position, and settled her right foot squarely on top of my left, where it remained for what felt like an eternity. This moment of euphoria created such a stir in my being that I bit my tongue so hard a warm trickle of blood flooded my mouth; I would have happily swallowed every drop of my own blood if it would have made that moment in paradise last.

I tried to play it cool, opting not to make direct eye contact right away. Instead, I went for the occasional side glance to see if I could catch a whiff of interest or intent. Was I one minute to midnight, the magical moment that I had longed for since I first cast eyes upon my sweet Ginger? Time ceased to exist. I had no comprehension of the words coming from Ms. Walter's mouth. And all the while, Ginger's foot remained atop of mine. I was just beginning to wonder if she had put it there by mistake when she tapped the sole of her shoe gently on the topside of mine.

Sweat flooded from my pores as my mind raced for a solution, and somehow Ms. Walters was expecting me to focus on the lesson. I had to snap back into reality—this was a reading group for God's sake. My parents had sent me to school to obtain an education and become a fine upstanding member of society, and here I was, wasting their hard-earned money, chewing the eraser off the end of my pencil as I sat, paralyzed, pondering my next course of action. All at once, my bubble of euphoria popped, and I came crashing back to earth. Reading group was over. Ginger's foot left mine as she stood to go with everyone else, and the loss of our physical connection snuffed out the ardent flame in my heart, leaving me cold and alone. Ms. Walters offered me a sympathetic glance and I knew that she understood the depths of my broken heart. I gathered my belongings, picked my pride and heartbreak up off the floor, and limped away, still pierced by Cupid's arrow.

That was the first and only true moment that Ginger and I shared during our entire fourth-grade year. However, I witnessed that day the power that love can possess. It can take the strongest of men and expose them on all fronts; a lesson that has resonated numerous times over the course of my life. That first love may have been innocent and inconsequential, but that did nothing to lessen the raw sting of a first heartbreak.

OH CHRISTMAS TREE

It was the first Saturday of December, a day bookmarked as one of my family's most important traditions: the hunt for the family Christmas tree. I am not sure how, when, or why this became such an integral part of our family's tradition, yet it served every year as the kickoff to our holiday season.

My parents had been priming the pump at dinner all week in preparation for our quest to find the perfect symbol of Christmas bliss. I recognized the importance of this necessary centerpiece, because all the rest of our holiday accessories were not to be set out until after our tree was in its rightful position. Any thought of decoration prior to the arrival of the tree was met with outright refusal. Being a boy who loved and lived for the sights and smells of the Christmas season, I always circled that first Saturday on my calendar. I loved the days leading up to Christmas, once the tree was decorated in full splendor and presents began to accumulate under the lowest limbs while the stockings slowly plumped with tiny treasures. Nevertheless, Christmas to me was always more about the magical month-long season, rather than the day itself. Christmas Day, as magnificent as it was, signified the beginning of the end, as the twinkling lights and colorful decorations gave way to the long gray wait till spring.

I never was one to sleep in as a youngster, not even on weekends, but it was always difficult to rouse myself that first Saturday of December after being kept up half the night with burning anticipation for the day ahead. Weather was always a factor in northeast Ohio, and my mother was adamant about her boys being prepared for the elements. Snow or not, long underwear was not optional. Neither were our thick wool socks, gloves, hats, scarves, or the multiple layers we were made to bundle into prior to leaving the home front. Within a half hour in the car, my brothers and I were roasting, attempting to surreptitiously shed layers in hopes of finding some temporary relief. The choice of transportation was our old brown station wagon, to which the interior ceiling fabric was stapled to keep it from drooping. She was a beauty as she rumbled down the interstate in search of this year's Christmas tree farm. I look back on that car with a genuine fondness and appreciation for the many family memories that were created in its confines. I couldn't have cared less what anyone else thought of our clunky working-class conveyance. It served as a reminder of all our parents had done to give us what we had, and as far as I was concerned, no fancy sports car could compare.

We never were privy to the location of the Christmas tree farm prior to the beginning of the drive. It was all part of the buildup—the place was never just up the street. The drive rarely lasted less than an hour, and no amount of are-we-there-yets could deter my parents from their chosen course. Only when at least one of us was on the verge of a full-blown meltdown did Dad suddenly pull the car over and declare that we had reached our promised land. In an instant, our frustrations were replaced with endless rows of massive Christmas trees as far as the eye could see. I always wondered where the hell my parents found out about these places, because never once did they to fail to live up to my holiday expectations.

We spent hours those first Saturdays of every December walking up and down the rows, inspecting Christmas tree after Christmas tree. But the initial excitement inevitably gave way to frustrated exhaustion as we struggled to agree on which tree to take home—a debate which became a family tradition in and of itself. My mother was given the final say, and I can remember her firm veto of a tree or two that was met with a volley of sighs and an outpouring of noisy protests. Yet our perseverance always paid off, and eventually we would settle on one that was deemed by all to be the perfect Christmas tree.

The next dilemma was that our chosen tree was invariably fields away from the parking lot, and we were forced to half-carry, half-drag it for what felt like miles back to the old station wagon. Finally, with rubber arms and frozen feet, my family would stagger back to wait with other exhausted holiday-goers while harried assistants rushed to help equally harried dads lash their trees to the roofs of their automobiles. At this point, I was always so exhausted that I would slump into the back seat and watch my father and some unknown man work magic with a rhythmic passing of twine back and forth over the mounted tree. A final handshake, some seasonal pleasantries, and within minutes we were on our way once more.

Exhausted from the whole ordeal, we generally dozed in the back of the car for most of the ride home, until we stopped for lunch on the way and got our second wind. With full bellies and renewed spirits, we would arrive home in the late afternoon hours to watch with fevered excitement as Dad and my older brother untied the tree from the top of the station wagon. The home stretch of the trip was moving the tree inside the house to take its final season-long resting place in the tree stand. The process was often met with excitement and unexpected drama. My mother would attempt to verbally guide the tree into the appropriate position while Dad muttered profanities from somewhere underneath the lowest boughs, which left my younger brother and I in fits of giggles as we sat by like excited puppies wagging our tails. When at last the tree was up, a cry of jubilation echoed throughout the house. Unfortunately, the night's festivities were concluded at that point as my brothers and I were reminded that the branches on the tree had to drop overnight. Who made up that rule?

So we sat all night and stared at that gigantic bush until exhaustion took us to sleep. We would awaken the next morning with the eager anticipation of finally being able to decorate the tree. And somehow, every year, we managed to forget that the next day was Sunday and Dad wasn't even going to string the lights until we got home from mass. 'Are you kidding me?' I would fume. We had this paramount task at hand and we had to go to church first? Surely given the occasion we could have a special dispensation, just this one Sunday? So went the arguments that my brothers and I bombarded our parents with, through the entire process of getting dressed and up to the moment we pulled into the church parking lot. Maybe it was just another stage of the family Christmas tree tradition? In any case, it was obvious that my parents were not interested in having this discussion with us and we mutinously trudged through the front entrance. I fidgeted from the opening hymn straight on through the homily, lost in fantasies of colored lights and shiny strands of tinsel. That mass marked one of the longest hours of the whole year, and we made no effort to disguise our impatience as the seconds dragged by. Communion offered a glimmer of hope, because that meant that mass was drawing to a close. If my brothers and I could hang on for just a few more minutes... Finally, the closing hymnal, and as our priest meandered down the main aisle of the church, I burst out in a triumphant, jubilant "Yes!" that caused my parents and several others to look over in wonder.

The first ornament each of us hung was the one my mother made or bought for us that year. It was part of the tradition, and Mom took great pride in making sure the ornaments were representative of each boy's personality. It usually took us a few hours to decorate the tree, and I am sure my parents had to do some late-night rearranging, but I was always mystified when we finished. It was the most magical weekend of the year. Before going to bed, I always took one last look around the decorated living room, shimmering by the light of our magnificent tree: the mantelpiece trimmed with garlands of pine, the stockings hung over the fireplace, the candles and decorations accumulated by our family through years of memories made together. I liked to cut the lights off and bask in the rosy glow of the string lights, allowing pride and fondness for my family to wash over me as I looked at all we had created together over the past couple days. Those moments, to me, are what Christmas is and should always be about, not the presents or even the morning itself.

The magic of the Christmas season is something that my wife and I work hard to recreate for our own two boys. We have each held on to some of the family traditions of old, and introduced a few new ones over the years, but our emphasis remains on love, warmth, and spending time together as a family. We can only hope to give them memories to cherish as we cherish our own, so that they may one day pass the true meaning of Christmas on to their own children.

THE MOVE OUT WEST

The writing was on the wall, but I was too young to realize that the move was going to take place as quickly as it did. All I knew was that the frustration in their voices when they talked over their post-Sunday-dinner coffee was mounting steadily, and had been for some time. My parents had spent every weekend for the better part of five months looking for a new house.

The fire that destroyed the two story fort my father had built for my brothers and me was the culminating event that pushed our eventual move out west, but it was by no means the first or only reason. I slept through the entire ordeal in which my father and a whole squad of firemen worked feverishly to extinguish the raging inferno in our backyard. Before the trucks arrived, my father had managed to severely burn a finger trying to fight the blaze on his own. But we weren't moving because of the fire. We were moving because we all knew damn well who had set it, and because proving it was next to impossible.

Our relationship with our next-door neighbors had been turbulent—that is to say, hellish—for the duration of the time we had lived on Dox Drive. The driving force behind the conflict was the family matriarch, a large and frankly trashy woman whose sole occupation, as far any of us could tell, was screaming abuse at her sons. I often felt sadness for those boys, though perhaps not as much as I might have had they not been the terror of the neighborhood, and my family in particular. The oldest, Nick, received the brunt of his mother's vitriol, and as a result reciprocated that negativity toward other neighborhood kids, especially Frank, my older brother. That said, many were the times myself and my younger brother, Jesse, happened to witness the tail end of one screaming match or another as Nick stormed out of his house, hurling profanities over his shoulder. We knew to make a hasty retreat inside on these occasions, as any convenient target would do when Nick was riled up. Relaying the information to our parents usually resulted in another shouting match between Nick's mother, my father, and Nick himself.

Nick's father was a passive man who in all truth I think feared his wife as much as his boys did. He never engaged in the turmoil either way, whether to defend his family's actions or condemn them. I remember once Frank planted sunflowers for our mom on Mother's Day. They grew to be about seven feet tall and were absolutely beautiful. My mother cherished those sunflowers and my older brother tended to their needs daily. I remember Nick threatening to cut the flowers down one day while my brothers and I were out playing on the front lawn. We never knew what fueled this particular outburst, but sure enough within a week, my mother's sunflowers were hacked to the ground. I remember watching her and my brother cry as my father's rage rocketed into an unparalleled stratosphere.

The ongoing conflict with our neighbors to the north had taken a toll on my family. But the fire, which we could only speculate was some form of retaliation for one slight or another, was the final straw. My father even paid for an eight-foot privacy fence to be constructed between the properties. It was difficult to listen to my parents vent their frustrations to each other with no viable solution. At the time, we lived on the outskirts of Cleveland, in an affordable neighborhood comprised predominately of blue-collar workers. We were moving to the suburbs, where my mother wanted to go, but it was going to be a huge leap of faith. My parents were both going to have to substantially increase their commutes to work, but our safety was their first priority. So we packed our bags, somehow managed to sell our house, and headed west into the great unknown.

During my last day of fourth grade, I struggled to keep it together as the bell rang, turning the page on this chapter of my life. All of a sudden, a girl named Mags ran up and handed me a homemade card. Before she ran out the door, she kissed my cheek and told me she was going to miss me. I read the card in which Mags professed how deeply she cared for me on the way out to the old station wagon, and as everyone cheered the end of the year, the first tears began to roll down my cheeks. I remember my father let me sit up front with him and I laid my head on his lap, continuing to cry for quite a while. Jesse, who was always a festive tyke, asked my father why I was so sad. Dad did his best to explain to him that I was upset to lose my friends, and he continued to tussle and rub my head for the entire car ride to our new home. Life is tough for a guy on the brink of fifth grade.

My family's great move westward took us approximately fifteen miles down I-480 to a quiet suburb outside of Cleveland. I have to say, the new neighborhood and house were all a ten-year-old-boy could hope for. I had my own bedroom for the first time in my life, and it came equipped with a locking door. Finally, I was going to be able to lip sync to my favorite tapes without fear of intrusion. Having recently developed a taste for music, my great ambition was to become a rock star. I liked to practice by dancing around my room and singing into an empty toilet paper tube for imagined hordes of screaming adolescents. I quickly learned the importance of closing my blinds and placing a towel at the bottom of the door before my performances. The neighborhood kids could easily see into my windows from our front yard, and Jesse loved to lie on his stomach and watch me embarrass myself through the crack under the door.

The neighborhood itself was made up of two cul-de-sacs at the end of a street that was occupied by children of all ages. That first summer, I spent many evenings well into twilight running around the block playing games of Kick the Can and Ghost in the Graveyard. Some nights were spent catching fireflies or just sitting on someone's porch, listening to the radio. There was a park only two blocks away, where I made a few friends playing in the local baseball league. Even the backyard pool, a hot commodity during a northeastern Ohio summer, was slightly larger than the one at our old house. For a short period of time, my life felt like something out of a book.

The days slowly whittled by, and before I knew it the dog days of summer were giving way to the early stages of autumn. The start of the school year was just around the corner, and my parents were feverishly pushing the idea of a new beginning. I wasn't buying it, nor was my little brother, Jesse, who was about to embark on his own maiden voyage into an official school setting.

As always, my parents worked, scraped, and somehow managed to find enough money to send my brothers and me to the local Catholic school. We lived a solid five miles away, so we were always the first students on the bus in the morning and the last ones dropped off in the afternoon. Thankfully, the bus we rode wasn't filled to capacity, and the neighborhood girl I had a crush on rode with us. However, it was quite apparent that I was invisible to her, as she sat confidently amongst the cool kids toward the back. I usually sat on the front bench with Jesse, assuming the role of family sentinel. Frank, who was establishing his independence, rode further back, away from his baby brothers. On that first day, I did my best to dry Jesse's tears, and when that didn't work, gave him a gentle kick in the ass as the bus rolled into the parking lot.

Frank, Jesse, and I were ready for a new start, so we packed our bags and headed west.

THE GOLDEN TICKET

Fifth grade was a year of transition and overeager efforts to fit in with my peers, which I decided would begin with my entering the student council election. I am not quite sure how or why I threw my hat into the ring. I've always embraced the necessity for service projects, such as food and clothing drives, which are fabulous. But I wasn't optimistic that this would be an asset to my résumé down the road.

But nonetheless, I threw caution to the wind and delivered my speech, along with the eight other students who decided this was a prime opportunity to improve their classroom status. Our school population was on a smaller scale compared to some of the local public schools, so being a part of the student leadership team was a tremendous honor. I sat in the back of the room next to one of the most unique kids I have ever met. His name was Dwayne, and the first time I met him he was wearing bowling shoes and had a dog collar around his neck. The bowling shoes, I was to learn, were his school shoes, and he wore them every day. The dog collar made an appearance every so often, but I never really understood the fashion statement. He still wore the polo and khakis required by the school, but he never failed to accessorize. I'm not certain why he latched onto me. Maybe it was because I was the new kid. I picked up on the sentiment that Dwayne was not well-liked by his peers, but whatever the reason, we soon developed a friendship.

Sister Kate was very explicit in her instructions that we were to cast only two votes each, and it was imperative that we vote for one boy and one girl. I thought this was a ridiculous rule—what about our rights under the Constitution? Casting the one vote for myself was a no-brainer, but I struggled to decide which girl to vote for. I had it down to MJ or a redhead named Katrina. I ultimately decided on MJ because I thought she was much more attractive, and if I was going to spend one lunch a week with someone, I would very much have liked to spend it with her. I had just finished folding my second vote when Dwayne leaned over and informed me that he had voted for me twice because he thought all of the girl candidates were horrible. I tried to surreptitiously admonish him, to remind him that we had to vote for one boy and one girl, but he just leaned back with a coy, smug smile on his face as if he had just pulled off the greatest bank heist of all time. I kept trying to get his attention, but every time I did Sister Kate would shush me. She was a stickler for due process, and reminded the class repeatedly that our votes were private and nobody else's business. That was easy for her to say, I thought to myself, after I had just learned that the entire election was compromised.

In the nature of a true election, Sister Kate called out the votes while one of my classmates tabulated the count on the board with tally marks. This of course did wonders for the self-esteem of the students who received only a few votes, yet for some reason I ended up a frontrunner as the early results came in. I was running hand in hand with a feller by the name of Mike, and from what little information I had been able to gather thus far in the school year, he was an extremely popular lad.

The girl vote was a blowout, with MJ running away with the competition. I suspect that she had swept the male vote. Back and forth, Mike and I battled as the votes dwindled down to the final few. And sure as eggs are eggs, I won the election by one vote. By one damn illegal vote, as cast by my new best friend, the class weirdo. Dwayne erupted into a jovial celebra-tion as if he was the one who had just been elected student council representative. But between his excessive celebration on my behalf and the jeering directed at the losing candidate, he had caught the attention of Sister Kate. She quickly rapped her yard stick on the chalk board, ending Dwayne's celebration prematurely. Oh, the moral dilemma to accept victory when I knew the accurate results had the election ending in a tie, or to raise my hand and explain to Sister Kate that the kid in the dog collar cheated and voted for me twice? My gut was telling me that this was all wrong and I should simply explain what happened to Sister Kate. Yet, in the back of my mind, I was worried about Dwayne becoming angry with me. After all, the whole point in my running had been to make friends, not enemies. It felt pretty lousy, but I decided my conscience could take the hit. So there I stood in the front of the class with the lovely MJ, as a fifth-grade student council representative.

Dwayne, odd as he was, provided me with my golden ticket to finding a niche amongst an already well-established class. Student council, well, it was what it was, and MJ took it a lot more seriously than I did. I wasn't crazy about the meetings occurring once a week during lunch and recess, yet I stuck it out, if for no other reason than most of the classes elected the beautiful people in their homeroom. It was Hollywood in miniature, elementary school style, so there was always plenty of eye candy to keep me visually involved in the discussions. MJ handled all of the reporting back to the homeroom while I stood next to her and simply nodded along. However, my status in our classroom society was slowly elevated, and for that I am truly thankful to Dwayne and his rigged election. I think my classmates actually thought that I had been granted more power by being elected than I actually had. Unfortunately, this was not the case, but I did enjoy the additional attention. Student suggestions came out of the woodwork and I brought them forward to the council, but most were unrealistic and shot down in relatively quick order. As the years went by, I saw less and less of Dwayne until he became another ghost in my life. Yet it is difficult to forget a guy who wore a polo button-down with a dog collar and bowling shoes with confidence. I never ran for student council again, maybe because I knew it would never stand up to my first run on the campaign trail. Truthfully, I had already experienced enough of the cut-throat world of the politics to last a lifetime.

POETIC IGNORANCE

Fifth grade was the first year I experienced switching classes, so I actually had two teachers. Ms. Shade, my social studies and language arts teacher, was young and fairly new to teaching. She struck me as the type of person who might have preferred to teach at a university, in that she made very little effort to hide her dislike of young people. She was arrogant and snobbish, and I disliked her as much as she disliked me.

My academic aptitude in fifth grade was not really worth writing home about, and Ms. Shade took every possible opportunity to remind me of that fact. I knew at a young age that any hopes of going to an Ivy League college were a lost cause. And so, toward the beginning of the holiday season, I started hanging out with a boy in my class named Jim.

Jim's father was a postman and had an extensive collection of nude magazines that he frequently kept in plain view on the basement bar. Jim had become an avid viewer of these magazines' pictures and was therefore knowledgeable in subject matter I had yet to even dream of. However, to his credit, he did his best to fill in the gaps in my spotty understanding of life sciences during long picture-walks through his dad's magazines. All the while, I was doing my best to determine what genre of literature they fell under. I'll admit that I was becoming increasingly aware of the girls in my classroom, and our recent introduction to "family life education" in health class had me tangled in knots.

We'd spent a few weeks learning the anatomy of both genders, which included an intense study of vocabulary and diagrams. It was a time of poorly-pronounced words and unsteady reading voices that gave way to numerous snickers during instruction. We were separated by gender during the family life classes, but the lessons were discussed in great detail between the sexes when we reconvened at lunch and recess. I knew absolutely nothing about adult relationships at this point in my life. My parents were my parents, and I never gave it a second thought as to how my brothers and I ended up on this earth. Unfortunately, my ignorance on the subject put me in quite a pickle one afternoon in early December.

On the day in question, my classmates and I found ourselves in the midst of a dreaded poetry lesson. I love poetry, but not in the way that Ms. Shade presented it to us. Her approach was so cut and dry, it resembled a lecture on algebra. We had been tasked with making our own couplets to teach us about rhyme schemes and meter. I hate poems that rhyme because they always seem to emphasize the rhyme itself and not the emotion. But there I was, doodling in my notebook as my classmates each stood in turn to present their poems, dreading my turn to share my own feeble effort (I can't stand the color of red / because it makes me dizzy in my head), when Jim, sitting behind me, tapped my shoulder and slipped me a piece of paper. Although the couplet written on the paper did rhyme, I wasn't sure what it meant or whether or not it actually made sense. But Jim, whispering over my shoulder, was insistent that I should read it out loud. I never asked why he was so excited for me to read his masterpiece, nor did I question why he didn't want to read the poem himself and take full credit. I shrugged it off and informed Jim that I would read his poem. Meanwhile, up and down the rows, our classmates continued to read their meaningless rhymes.

Finally, it was my time to shine. As I stood to proclaim Jim's poetic masterpiece as my own, I noticed that Jim had put his head down on his desk, his shoulders shaking uncontrollably.

Logic should have stopped me at that moment, but I went ahead with it anyway. I took a deep breath and belted out my line:

"Don't be sad on this fine day / because today you are going to get laid."

The look of horror on my teacher's face, combined with the outburst of laughter from some of my peers, made me realize I was in deep trouble. When Jim finally raised his head from the cross of his forearms, his face had gone several shades of red from trying to suppress his laughter. I was quickly ushered into the hallway, where Ms. Shade proceeded to give me the verbal ass-chewing of my life. She went on for what felt like hours about how I should be ashamed of myself for proclaiming such vulgarities in a classroom setting, and who did I think I was, making a mockery of her poetry lesson? What would my parents think if they knew this was the content of my poem? Was this Christian language? I stood there absorbing the blows without a word of rebuttal, because I truthfully had no idea what the hell I had just said.

Upon returning to my desk, I cordially extended my middle finger toward Jim as he continued to suppress his giggles through the remainder of our afternoon classes. It became the talk of the fifth grade, and I was terrified that Sister Kate was going to find out and send me on a one-way trip to visit Padre over at the church's confessional. The remaining few minutes of the day dragged on as I looked for solace at the bottom of an empty seat on the bus. However, word of my carnal ignorance had spread like the plague, and I was forced to endure another hour of ridicule during the long ride home.

I exited the bus and walked up my driveway with a steady flow of tears rolling down my cheeks. Once inside I sped up to my bedroom, locked the door, and wept inside my closet for the next hour until my mother came looking for me. From my classmates' many whisperings, I had gained a more thorough understanding of what my poem meant, and I was ashamed to tell her for fear that she would wash my mouth out with soap. Fifth grade boys weren't supposed to talk about getting laid, especially in a parochial classroom, and I was certain hell was coming for me. My mother coaxed me out of the closet and sat down with me on my bed. She was gentle in her questioning as to why I was so upset. My parents wanted us to be the best we could be, and to make them proud in all avenues of our lives. I knew in my heart that I had let them down. I would have rather confessed my sin to a priest at that point than to have to disappoint my mother. I conjured up the courage and blurted out my poetic vulgarity, then waited for the gates of damnation to swallow me whole. Instead, all I heard was my mother's soft laughter.

God bless my mother. We talked for over an hour about my poetic mishap and how I should holster that topic for the foreseeable future. She then proceeded to write my teacher a note explaining my ignorance of the topic of sex. Ms. Shade looked at me in disbelief when I delivered it. To this day she probably thinks that I was another class comedian who pulled the wool over his parents' eyes. I learned many valuable life lessons during my time as a fifth-grade poet. Most importantly, that I still had a lot to learn about life.

FIRST DATE

Following the poetry debacle, winter break of fifth grade found me out on my first official date, although I was adamantly opposed to the idea. Debbie was a friend of mine from my previous school. I remember that she was intelligent, kind, and generally quite likeable. She had always been someone I felt comfortable with. I knew she missed me after I left at the end of fourth grade, because our mothers had exchanged phone numbers and she called me occasionally to check in. Debbie was the sort of friend that one could always count on, but she had never pushed any of my romantic buttons. To my understanding, the date was her idea, which her mother passed along to my mother over the phone. Thus, it was all arranged. Thankfully, this was only to be a quick trip to the Pizza Hut and maybe a time or two around the skating rink. I was living out west now, so I had to be driven back to my old stomping grounds. Mom dropped me off at Debbie's house and we were chauffeured to the local Pizza Hut by Debbie's mother, who instructed us to call her when we were ready to be picked up. I got out of the car and immediately started looking for a payphone, but Debbie caught my eye before I could make good my escape.

So, I backtracked a step or two and proceeded to hold the door open for my date. I may not have been particularly enthusiastic about all this, but a gentleman is a gentleman. Upon the arrival of our waitress, I was quick to whip out my wallet, which contained two certificates, each good for one personal pan pizza. I dramatically laid them on the table and was sure to give her the all-important head nod to ensure she was reading my cards correctly. She made quite the spectacle of the fact that I had read for two whole months to earn these certificates, and remarked that the lady seated across from me must have been extremely special. I did in fact read for two whole months, a grand total of eight books. I had recently graduated to chapter books thanks to the sports fiction of Matt Christopher. I shot the waitress another look so that she knew to slow her roll, but the damage was already done. Debbie was beaming from ear to ear and I knew that in all likelihood my lips were not going to get out of this evening without seeing some sort of action.

As we waited for our food to come out, we chatted about this and that, mainly my new school and some of our old classmates. It took about ten minutes for those topics to run their course, however, from which point on the meal was nothing short of disastrous. After long minutes of awkward silence peppered with forced conversation, I started picking up on a vibe from Debbie that made me distinctly uncomfortable. It was like she wanted us to be something that we weren't, although in fifth grade that was extremely difficult for me to fully comprehend, much less vocalize. She'd reach out across the table to hold my hand and I would politely pull it away. She would make exaggerated eye contact with me while licking her lips. I would take a long pull of soda through my straw and stare intently at the ice in my glass. It felt fake, and forced, and it upset me because I didn't want to hurt Debbie's feelings. Even though I had never been on a date, I had a feeling that this wasn't a model for a love connection.

We finally left the Pizza Hut and ventured out, not knowing what the blustery December evening would hold. We were only a few blocks away from my old school, in a small shopping center that housed a few chain restaurants and stores. Across the street was an ice-skating rink, which stood adjacent to an arcade. We opted not to go ice-skating, but instead walked, sweaty-hand-in-hand, over to the arcade, only to find that it was closed, further adding to the misery of the evening. I guess we could have gone ice-skating instead, but I was and still am terrible on ice skates. Besides which, I was kind of getting antsy to end our date.

It wasn't that I disliked Debbie, but I had no idea what I was doing when it came to ladies. It was that feeling of uncertainty that drew me back into a persistent state of awkward shyness over the course of the date. As cell phones were the stuff of science fiction at this point in history, Debbie had arranged for us to be picked up in an hour or so. Maybe it was the cold or the guilt of disappointing my date, but I finally mustered up the courage to place my arm over Debbie's shoulder to provide some chivalrous warmth. I knew the action was going to be misconstrued, but damn it, I was cold. We cuddled in an extremely awkward manner for several minutes before we turned to face each other. Debbie leaned in, head turned slightly to the side, eyes closed as though she had been in this moment before. Not counting my traumatic kindergarten encounter with Carrie, I had only kissed my mother, grandmother, and aunts at this point in my life, and none of them ever turned their heads and closed their eyes when they kissed me. I tried to follow suit, turning my head slightly in the opposite direction, but I kept my eyes open. I was afraid I may miss her lips and end up kissing her nose or chin. In a single, off-beat, cinnamon-scented moment, our lips locked, separated, and locked again. No fireworks went off. As soon as it had begun, it was over, and we were headed back to the Pizza Hut to wait for Debbie's mom.

We shared a Coke in silence, uncomfortably interlocking our fingers on the ugly red vinyl table cloth. It wasn't love, of that I was certain, but the simple innocence of that moment has always stayed with me. Debbie's mom drove me back out west, traversing through a lightly falling snow. When we arrived, I bid Debbie's mom goodnight and gave Debbie's shoulder a light squeeze. I looked back as I opened the door to see the station wagon pulling out of the driveway, and I offered a half-hearted wave. I'm not sure if Debbie saw it or waved back, but I never saw or heard from her again. Funny, how one minute a person can be part of your life, and the next they become ghosts, still walking amongst the living.

My own sons are getting older. Emmett is entering second grade and Sawyer is heading into kindergarten. It is interesting and somewhat comical to observe their interactions with their peers and how drastically things have changed since just a few short years ago. I wonder how I will handle the idea of their first date. The thought has crossed my mind. Society moves at such a rapid pace these days, and I'm watching these two boys and their generation growing up way too quickly. I try to take from my own experiences and apply it in a positive manner when helping them to navigate the challenges they encounter as they grow. I can only hope that they hold out for that first date until they are truly ready for it. Time will tell.

DETENTIONS AND HEARTACHE

In the fall of sixth grade, I made a name for myself as a hard hitting, lightning fast two-way player on the fifth-and-sixth-grade football team. I was the starting slot back on offense and started at left cornerback on the defense side. Although I had no formal experience prior to that year, having only played backyard football up to that point, I found I enjoyed the game well enough. But the best asset by far was the attention my play on the gridiron brought me from my peers. Unfortunately, it also brought out my devious side, and it wasn't long before I received my first detention.

The behavioral expectations of parochial school were stringent, and I had been pushing my luck for a while with my disruptive attempts to establish myself as class comedian. I don't remember what it was that caused Ms. Hollins to reach her breaking point in the end—something stupid, undoubtedly— but I do remember that when she finally snapped, time stopped cold. The entire class sat in paralyzed silence as my judgment was handed down, and I felt my insides liquefy at the thought of my father's inevitable wrath. My mother's disappointment was nothing to be trifled with, but even her shouting couldn't hold a candle to my pops when he was riled. He prided himself on raising boys who were respectful of their elders, especially because he and my mother worked their asses off to give us a private school education. I was in for it when I got home.

The actual writing of the detention slip was a production in and of itself; the action of Ms. Hollins removing the slip from the top drawer, the overemphatic scrawling of her pen across the carbon copy form, and the final tearing of the perforated top copy stretched out in a moment of isolation that lasted an eternity, followed by the unfathomable walk of shame as I made my way to the desk to accept my punishment, fluttering in the air between my teacher's fingers. Even the smell of the detention slip burned a lasting impression on my soul as I tucked it into my take-home folder.

In detentions to come, I was to learn that the aftermath was largely dependent upon the time of day the incident took place. Detentions received at the end of the school day were horrific for a multitude of reasons. There was no time to receive the accolades of one's peers, and it left one with very little time to formulate an excuse for one's parents. In later years, I was usually pissed off about the fact that I had made it so close to the end of the day, only to find myself in trouble right before the bell rang. But a detention received early in the day was often revered amongst my classmates, rendering me a James Dean of the sixth grade. I won't lie; I fed off of the attention of that first detention and relished it. However, I also came to learn that having the entire day to develop and rehearse a good explanation for my folks just gave the dread of facing them all the more time to build. Every second that passed inched me closer to my doom.

Detentions were served the day after they were received immediately after school and lasted a half hour. No excuses, no matter what family or personal conflicts interfered, and in those days, parents backed teachers come hell or high water. My parents never wanted to hear my side of the story. We were raised to respect authority, not to question it. My house was five miles from the school, and almost every time I received a detention I was left to walk home. It was part of my punishment: if I was going to be an inconvenience to my classmates and teachers, then I was going to be inconvenienced with a long walk carrying a heavy book bag.

A detention also usually equated to a week's grounding at home. School nights consisted of nothing more than dinner and an evening in my room. My radio was removed from my bedroom, and I never had my own television, so my options for entertainment were fairly limited. I could read a book or sit on my bed and contemplate the error of my ways. I wasn't much of a reader until college, so I spent a lot of time hanging upside down from the side of my bed looking at the gigantic swatch watch hanging on my wall. Weekends were not a whole lot different. I was not permitted to play outside with my brothers or friends. Television was off-limits and strictly enforced. My only shot at outside time was if my parents wanted me to do some yard work. It was the real deal when I messed up, and my parents made sure I knew it was unacceptable.

So it went for the remainder of sixth grade and into my seventh-grade year. I would get myself into enough trouble to receive a detention, and then I would fly straight for a while. It became a cyclical pattern of behavior that year, and one that not only disappointed my parents, but myself as well.

It was on one of those long post-detention walks home that I tasted my first cigarette. A fellow rabble-rouser, known around school as Picker, was walking home with me, having shared time in the hole that afternoon. I was in for public flatulence—go figure—right in the middle of religion class, while Picker's offence was an accumulation of disrespectful outbursts throughout the day. Picker lived a few miles from me, but at least I had company for half the walk. As we walked, he led me on what he claimed was a shortcut through a classmate's yard, which was supposed to shave some time and distance off of our journey—all of which was a lie, as I was soon to find out. In truth, we were dropping by only to lift a pack of smokes off said classmate's old man. He was a well-known chain smoker amongst the parishioners in the church community, and his son, Chuck, who was not especially well liked, often bragged to the other boys in class about smoking his father's cigarettes on the sly.

And wouldn't you know it, there was Chuck, smoking a cigarette as he opened the door to let us in. Our shortcut cost us an additional thirty minutes of random chit-chat as Picker scoped the joint and plotted his heist. My primary role in all of this nonsense was to sidetrack Chuck in any way possible. So I went on the grand tour of Chuck's house, listening to him ramble on about each room as if we were touring some famous museum. The air was rancid with the smell of stale tobacco, and around each corner was another ash tray filled with the remnants of snuffed out butts. Chuck was extremely proud of his father's bowling trophies and the hall of family pictures that spanned his life from birth to his current seventh grade photo. Afterward, Picker and I bid Chuck farewell as we navigated our way through the dog's landmines in his backyard and scrambled over the chain link fence. Picker was seriously hooked on nicotine, because we were barely out of Chuck's sight when he tore into that pack of cigarettes like a starving man opening a twinkie. Picker had a collection of lighters he'd lifted stashed in the smaller pouch of his JanSport backpack. I watched as he took two long puffs, incinerating half of the cigarette in the process before exhaling a fog of smoke that left me temporarily blinded.

Picker lit me up a smoke, to which I thankfully obliged him, but in truth had no idea what to do with. About halfway through my first cigarette, Picker informed me that I was reverse smoking. Instead of inhaling the smoke, I was blowing into the filter, thus watching the cherry glow at the end of the cigarette. What the hell did I know? But I sure found out the difference the first time I inhaled, because I nearly hacked up my left lung. It brought Picker to tears and infuriated me to the point that I decided I was going to finish this cigarette or die trying. I did, and I hated every excruciating drag. Even though we were in the same grade, I kind of looked up to Picker. He was extremely popular in our school for his amazing abilities as a guitar player, and he carried himself with an air of confidence that commanded everyone's attention. We were casual acquaintances, primarily due to the fact that we rode the same bus, but our friendship blossomed during our times in detention together. I had impressed Picker enough that I found acceptance into his realm of cool, which was all I craved at that particular time in my life. We walked along for the next mile or so in relative silence as Picker proceeded to smoke half the pack of cigarettes. I bid Picker farewell when we parted ways and spent the rest of the walk smelling my own breath and trying to figure out a way to cover the smell before I made it home.

I'm no expert in the field of psychology, but I would gamble that there was a correlation between my onslaught of detentions and the beginning of what I interpreted as the first of my parents' more serious marital disputes. I was aware at the time that all married couples go through their fair share of spats; my parents had been no different during the early part of my childhood. I am now fully aware of the unexpected stresses that marriage and family can heap on a person. Being married now for twelve years and having two young boys of my own, every day is a test of patience, and some days I am more successful than others as I attempt to learn from my mistakes and strive to make improvements for tomorrow. Yet nothing could ever compare to the first time I heard my father's voice pierce the silence and darkness of the night, causing me to sit up so quickly I was certain that I had soiled my britches in my sleep.

Now, I had heard my father angry before—more often than not at me or my brothers and our latest hijinks. However, this was a different, more intense level of anger in his voice. I sat there motionless at some early hour, clinging to every word of the argument my parents were engaged in somewhere in the lower level of our home. My father's voice had an edge that cut through any defense my mother offered. I cowered against my headboard in a seated position with my comforter pulled up around me for a false sense of protection. Within a few minutes, the yelling and slamming of doors had awakened my younger brother to a sense of fear echoed in his muffled crying. I left the safety of my bedroom and crawled frantically down the darkened hallway in order to offer some sort of assurance, but my feeble attempts at comfort only lasted a few moments as the cries of her youngest son reached my mother's ears. She threw the emotional well-being of her children in my father's face as she ascended the stairs to console my brother.

Mom and Dad—young, beautiful and in love.

Thirty years later, through a multitude of conversations with both my parents, I now have better insight into the financial and personal stresses they were dealing with during this time. It can be a living hell trying to support a family of three boys, maintain a healthy marriage, and still find the necessary time to satisfy one's own personal goals and needs, and I have yet to meet a person in all my years who has been able to juggle all the demands of life consistently without dropping the ball somewhere along the line.

In my own marriage, I've observed the negative effects that our arguing has on my own boys. It stems from two very different perspectives on life; that of adulthood in all its stressful splendor, and that of an innocent child who has yet to experience the hardships that come part and parcel with life in the real world. I am learning that communication between all members of the family is paramount. My boys don't need to understand all of the factors of their parents' arguments, but we've found that offering them insight into why people disagree can go a long way in helping them understand how to express their displeasure in a healthy way. Families argue. It's inevitable; living in close proximity with anyone for a prolonged period of time is going to push buttons, and we're no different. But I think it is important for my boys to understand the reasons behind the argument, at least to a degree that is appropriate for their age. My parents never discussed their arguments with us. Frank and I were old enough to make our own inferences, but we never sat down as a family to discuss what was truly going on. I do my best to reassure my boys that people disagree, even people who love each other. The source of the disagreement is not necessary for them to comprehend at their age, but I want them to understand the importance of communicating through disputes. It is an imperative skill that they need to be able to apply to their own lives.

An eerie silence settled in the aftermath of that first fight, with only the shushing sound of my mother's voice, barely audible from my brother's bedroom, registering in my ears. In that one night, my idyllic home life was shattered. The fights continued and escalated from there, with long tense silences lasting a week or two, every morning leaving us scared that today would be the day it would all blow up again.

My long walks home from detention gave my thoughts ample opportunity to drift between brooding over the situation at home and wallowing in the idealistic world that I wished more than anything I could return to.

"Hey kid, what are you doing?"

"What?"

"You're standing on my lawn."

Looking around, I realized the truth of the total stranger's observation. Distracted by thoughts of my parents' most recent fight, I had stopped walking altogether, and only God and that stranger can say how long I had been standing there. When I finally made it home, I rushed upstairs to vigorously brush my teeth and hide my clothes in the bottom of the hamper, too naïve not to be paranoid in my rule-breaking. My parents never noticed the smell.

HARD KNOCKOFF LIFE

My behavior that year continued to spiral downward, and combined with the emotional baggage that I was carrying due to the conditions at home, my mental state could best be described as a train wreck. The move out west had been the right choice overall, but the financial stresses it caused for my parents were very apparent. I had watched my father sit down after many a Sunday dinner with a cup of coffee, his checkbook, and a notepad that he used to calculate our monthly budget. It usually foreshadowed an argument when my mother would sit down to join him shortly afterward, her own cup of coffee in hand. Make no mistake, my parents wanted what was best for their boys. They both worked tirelessly to provide us with all that they could. But keeping our heads above water was extremely taxing on them. One of the most polarizing realities that I have learned over my years of adulthood and parenthood is that the financial burdens of everyday life are an albatross around most peoples' necks, even if they try to hide it. My parents always did their best to keep us in the loop of the latest fashion, but the financial reality of raising three boys often did not allow for us to purchase the name-brand gear. I wore shoes out faster than my parents could purchase new ones.

My mother was always on my case about wearing down the backs of my tennis shoes, because I refused to untie them and put them on properly. I would just squish down the back and wiggle my foot inside, and the size of my big toe combined with my slightly pigeon-toed walk always led to a hole in rather quick fashion. So needless to say, the idea of my parents buying me new Nikes every six weeks was totally out of the question. We rarely went to the mall except to window shop and kill time, and we always came home with minimal purchases. Our primary clothing-and-shoe outlet was a store known as Hills, which was a slight step up from K-Mart but definitely not in the same esteemed company as the local department store. Many families shopped at Hills. It was a huge place. My favorite part was that they had a snack counter that sold slushies and hot pretzels. I never thought twice about how others might perceive the quality of clothing that came from Hills.

But no individual is exempt from the reign of ridicule, regardless of their popularity. I jumped headfirst into the fads of fashion throughout my childhood, from cowboy boots to cuffed jeans, doc shoes, and even the high-top phase. Michael Jordan's legendary abilities had made Nike high-tops the craze of my day. Now, there was no way that I was ever going to be the owner of a pair of Air Jordans, but I was certain that the Jordache high-tops sold at Hills would make the cut. They were all white and trimmed in black with black lettering, and they rocked a printed pattern on the side wall. When the time once again came for my tennis shoes to be replaced, my mother at last indulged me and brought me to Hills to pick out a pair. We went on a Sunday evening, but in the world of Catholic school, the only time tennis shoes were permitted was during gym class, which didn't come around until Thursday. So unfortunately, the world was going to have to wait until then to see my prized possessions.

My school did not have a gym locker room, so the boys and girls changed separately, usually in the bathroom or in the classroom prior to the start of gym class. This week found us changing in the health classroom due to our poor choices in the boy's bathroom the week prior. Left unsupervised and in various stages of undress, we had decided that the bathroom was an ideal place to test out our chicken fighting skills. The game consisted of two teams of two—one boy sitting on the other's shoulders—and the object was simple: the two guys on top duked it out in a no-holds-barred death match, while the two on the bottom maintained a steady base for the top guys. Meanwhile, the rest of the boys formed a crude ring to shout encouragements at the competitors. The match ended when one of the top guys was sent crashing to the filthy bathroom floor. We had many an epic battle over the course of several weeks, and it likely would have lasted the remainder of the year had one fight the previous week not gone slightly awry.

Over the course of these battles, Picker and I had become the team to beat. Picker was strong and about a foot taller than me, so he made up the foundation of our team. I was scrappy, tenacious, and on the wrestling team, to say nothing of having two brothers. Together, we upended many a challenger, before finally meeting our match. We were locked in a seesaw battle that had been going back and forth across the bathroom floor for a couple minutes, when Picker lost his balance and sent me and my opponent, a kid named Danny, crashing through the end stall. Determined not to break our winning streak, I made sure to drag Danny along with me as we broke through the wall. Needless to say, the gym teacher was none too pleased with the noise, or damage to the bathroom. More infuriating still, no matter how she or the principal shook down the whole lot of us, not a single boy ratted us out. We stood our ground as a unit, and as a result, lost our bathroom changing privileges.

So it was there that I struggled to control my excitement as I pulled my new Jordaches out of my gym bag as my classmates changed quickly into the silky red shorts and white t-shirts that comprised our gym uniforms.

The atmosphere of a boy's locker room is like a festering pimple of immaturity that explodes and continues to ooze for the full five minutes that it takes to change clothes. Wisecracks about body type, hygiene, and choice of underwear flew indiscriminately, and those who started puberty early made sure that everyone knew about it. I myself was an easy target due to my skinny frame, meager peach fuzz, and hand-me-down drawers. But I had the Jordache high-tops, and so today, for once, I would be the envy of all of my classmates. Or so I thought.

Pulling my gems out of my bag, I began to nonchalantly pull them on, glancing around out of the corner of my eyes as I waited for my classmates to notice. It didn't take long. Suddenly, I heard Danny's voice from across the classroom.

"What the hell kind of shoes are those?"

That was all it took for the onslaught to begin.

"Hey nice rip-offs, man."

"What's the matter, your parents can't buy you the real deal?"

"Excuse me, butt-breath," I fought back furiously like a cornered animal. The boys were really letting me have it, but I was giving them back as much verbal tongue lashing as I had in my arsenal. It wasn't the ridicule that I minded so much but the blow to my family's financial status. My self-esteem was six feet underground before I made it to the hallway.

The jokes kept on coming as we lined up next to the girls to head toward the gymnasium. As if matters weren't bad enough, the girls caught wind of the jokes and added to my embarrassment with a steady stream of smirks and giggles. I walked into the gym feeling like I was wearing clown shoes. Physical education was usually my favorite subject, but not that day. We were playing field hockey, and I staked out the far goal and remained there for the duration of class. At least it kept me away from my classmates as they chased the plastic puck around the gym. I kept my head down and tried to not to draw any more jeers, and made sure I was the first one dressed after class, quickly tucking away my despicable shoes into my gym bag. The day dragged on in a sea of embarrassment that felt like an eternity. Gym class was only second period and I was forced to endure the verbal onslaught for the remainder of the school day.

I meandered down the driveway that afternoon, lagging behind my brothers as the school bus pulled away from our house. Instead of walking in the front door, I opened the garage and made my way to our trash cans. I lifted the lid, pulled out my new shoes from my school bag, and hid them under several bags of garbage. A few days later, my mom observed me wearing my old, ratty tennis shoes and inquired as to the whereabouts of my new Jordaches. Holding back tears, I weakly shrugged my shoulders before I bolted for the comfort of my bedroom. My mother, thankfully, left it alone.

BIG RED AND ESCALATED DRAMA

It was a splatter of ketchup across the normally subdued misfits' lunch table that started it all. At the end of my seventh-grade year, my parents and I sat down with the principal at my parochial school for a meeting about my behavior. It was suggested—or rather, mandated—that a change of scenery would be in my best interest. So, I was invited to transfer into a public middle school at the beginning of eighth grade. I was terrified with the idea of making new friends, and worried that my obsessive-compulsive fidgeting routine would draw the attention of my peers. It took me well into early spring to finally befriend a few fellas through my classes. Fortunately, I ended up sharing the same lunch period as them. Up until then, I had spent the first three quarters eating in relative solitude at the far end of the cafeteria with all the other friendless loose ends. The new crew that had welcomed me to break bread with them were hardly in the upper echelons of the middle school pecking order themselves, but as the skinny new kid, I counted my blessings for even this level of acceptance.

My acceptance, such as it was, could best be described as "tolerated." For a fortnight I sat quietly at the end of the misfit table and did my best to make valuable contributions to the proceedings, and while nobody went out of their way to make me feel welcome, they didn't try to make me feel unwelcome either. One fella, whom I fondly called "Big Red," sat in the middle of the table and displayed a stoic quietness that I found mildly intimidating. I had observed him in the hallways, but we had never had class together, much less struck up a conversation.

All I knew was that he was a transplant from central Ohio and that he'd developed quite a reputation as a tenacious football player. Big Red's broad shoulders, pale Irish skin, and red afro played into his mystique. But on this day, it transpired that I found myself sitting right across from Big Red, cowed into an awkward silence by his looming presence, until he asked with perfect courtesy if he might have one of my French fries. Maybe it was nerves, or just the whiskey courage of having friends to show off for again after almost a year in solitude. Whatever the reason, I considered the fry in my hand for a fraction of a second, and then, like a man possessed, let it fly across the table to smack Big Red squarely below the left eye. The horrified silence around the table was almost palpable.

It took Big Red all of an instant to reach across the table, take another one of my fries, dip it in my ketchup, and return fire, covering my new t-shirt in a red splatter to make Jackson Pollock proud. All I could do was laugh, because to challenge Big Red to a fight was a certain death sentence. In the end all I could do was shake Big Red's hand and share the remainder of my fries with him. And thus, a friendship that would span the next twenty-five years was formed.

A week later baseball season started, and lo and behold, there at the field for our first practice was Big Red. We both shook our heads in disbelief and chuckled at the implausibility of our predicament. It only took one practice for the whole team to realize that Red was by far the superior out of all of us. He became our go-to pitcher and spent the remainder of the games behind the plates, calling the game for the other pitchers. I bounced between second base and center field, due primarily to my inconsistent throwing ability and confidence after fielding balls in the infield. I never had any problem making the plays in the field, but something always got into my head before I threw the ball to first, resulting in alarming inaccuracy.

In any case, Big Red, whether out of sympathy, loneliness,

or the sheer proximity of our homes, took pity on me—sorry excuse for a ball player that I was—and we started to hang out. Initially, it was nothing more than me riding my bike over to Red's house to play video games for an hour or two after school. Big Red had a Sega Genesis, and we spent the majority of our time playing sports games. Truthfully, I hated every minute of it because even then I thought video games were pointless, (though I did kind of like that Sonic the Hedgehog character). But mostly, I was just thankful to have a new friend. Little did I know, what had begun as a convenient camaraderie would soon develop into a near-brotherly bond, as I came to lean on Red more and more over the summer and into our freshman year of high school.

The dynamic duo of Big Red and myself, caught up in an early autumn pose-off of masculinity.

As my friendship with Red grew, so did the frequency of my parents' arguments. Summer brought us freedom from the obligations of school, but it did not pardon me from the vivid hardships of my parents' deteriorating relationship, which hung over our house like a dreadful plague. There was no rhyme or reason to what could set them off. Money was a constant concern, as was Mom's new position at the hospital where she worked. My brothers and I spent the summer walking on eggshells, ready at a moment's notice to get out of the way should another fight break out. To their credit, upset as they were, our parents did their best not to directly involve us.

The most peaceful hours of the summer were those my parents spent at work, leaving Jesse and I in the nurturing, if somewhat overbearing care of Frank, whom I'm fairly certain felt a tremendous sense of pride at being deemed responsible enough to look after his two kid brothers. Still, we dreaded the three o'clock hour, when our father would come home, soon to be followed by our mother, and God only knew what the evening would bring.

I sought refuge in my evening baseball games and the kindness of Big Red, who was more than willing to let me sleep over multiple nights a week. It almost became routine that after a ball game, I would return home to get cleaned up and then hop on my ten-speed for a night at his place. I always hated to leave Jesse, because I never knew if that was going to be the night that the tinderbox would go up. Yet the thought of enduring another shouting match was always enough to send me out the door.

Secretly, I think my parents were quite relieved that I had found a safe place away from the chaos. They knew how sensitive I was and how deeply I felt the pain of their arguments. On those nights at Red's house, we would play his video games, watch Saturday Night Live reruns, talk about girls, and eventually fall asleep on the two adjacent couches in his living room. However, the thought of Jesse and my parents haunted me constantly. I remember offering up a prayer to God each night before I fell asleep on Red's couch to keep my brothers safe and let peace prevail that night in my family's household. Many nights it did, and some nights it did not. I will forever be grateful to Red's mom, because whether she gained insight from my parents, through Red's secondhand accounts of my family situation, or simply had a mother's intuition, she always let me sleep over whenever Red asked.

Those arguments have stayed with me for the better part of thirty years, and at the time they were never far from my thoughts. The most recent fights would replay themselves in the middle of class, on the bus, and every other moment in between. Perhaps most frustrating of all was that, when my parents weren't fighting, we were a textbook example of an all-American family. We went on vacations, celebrated holidays, played, laughed, and genuinely enjoyed each other's company. For a while, things would start to feel like they were on the mend. My parents had a genuine and heartfelt love toward each other. They had met when they worked together during the Christmas season at a local dime store known as Uncle Bills. My mother was attempting to help my father take an artificial Christmas tree down from the top shelf for a customer, when my father lost his grip and dropped the tree on her. I'm not sure if the customer still wanted the tree after that, but my father felt terrible and decided to ask my mother out to make it up to her. They married quite young, but so did a lot of people back then. I loved to listen to their stories about their families and respective upbringings. I knew their songs on the radio and would giggle in the backseat when they sang them to each other. We spent a lot of time going to family barbeques and birthday parties, especially on my father's side. He was one of six brothers and the extended family took every opportunity they could to get together. I have countless happy memories of my family and the wonderful times we shared together. When times were good, there was nowhere else in the world I'd have rather been than with my family.

Still, always persistent in the back of my mind was the worry of when the next fight was going to start. The good times never lasted that long, usually a few weeks at a time, and then the bottom would fall out again. And when it did, the effects on all of us and our ability to function normally were immediate and devastating.

The initial sign of a fight was always the sight of my father bringing a pillow and blanket to the living room couch. We rarely knew at that moment what the argument was about, but we always found out later that night. Fear always led to long nights of insomnia, and I would struggle to stay awake during school the following day. When I was able to keep my eyes open during class, my thoughts were never on the lesson.

Of course, there was no way I was going to let on to anyone, least of all my parents, how much pain I carried with me on a daily basis. I tucked it away for decades' worth of rainy days, hoping that one day I would come to grips with the deterioration of my happy home life. The most embarrassing times were when the neighbors would ask questions: "Is everything alright over there?" I really wanted to turn to them and yell, "What the hell do you think?" Instead, I usually opted for the all is well head nod before disappearing through the front door. Oh, how I prayed for my parents to find peace with each other.

BASEBALL

There was never a doubt in my mind that baseball was the most sacred of all sports. I loved everything about the game. My dad used to keep an old work radio in the garage. I had no earthly idea how old it was and cared little that the antenna was busted. It was speckled with paint from supervising a variety of my father's projects over the years, and the reception was intermittently interrupted with static, which I always thought was part of its mystique. I would sit and listen to the Cleveland Indian ballgames every chance I got, and drift away on the radio waves to fields far beyond the municipal stadium down on the Erie, where the crowd would erupt in thunderous cheers as I took my late-inning homerun trot around the backyard, hands raised to the sky. In reality, the Indians lost over a hundred

games during the summers of the mid 1980's, but I never cared about their record. I wore their hats, collected their baseball cards, idolized their players, and spent countless hours eating peanuts while I listened to them lose a heart-breaker in the late innings on that old radio.

There is much to say for the way the web of a raw-hide leather glove smells as it's pressed against your face,

If I could, I would have spent every moment of my youth between the lines of the diamond.

waiting for the outcome of the next pitch, or the comfort to be found in that same web after making an error that costs your team a meaningful moment in a game, sheltering you from the embarrassment of your mistake. The beauty in baseball is that each pitch provides a new beginning, and an opportunity to rectify a previous error. The smell of that beautiful, dusty glove that I slapped against my upper thigh could make me feel like I was ten feet tall after somehow managing to track down that fly ball after it was sent into temporary orbit by the opposing team. I tightened the laces with my teeth and smacked that pocket with my fist throughout each game I played over the course of thirteen spring and summer seasons.

When it came to the box, I always preferred a handful of dirt to batting gloves, even during those early spring games when the temperature sometimes never made it above forty degrees. I knew the metallic bat was going to sting like hell if I caught up to a fastball on one of those days, but it was always necessary for me to feel the leather of the bat handle. There was something authentic about the way that my callused hands wrapped around the grip. I don't imagine most pitchers I faced during those summers would have categorized me as intimidating when I stepped up to the plate. I was a scrawny, scrappy player, never batting higher than sixth in the order until I hit puberty and gained some muscle. I often pulled my head out when I swung at a pitch, and solid contact usually consisted of a single dropped over the heads of the drawn-in infielders. But occasionally I would connect on a pitch that would find its way to the gap, and leave me standing on second base feeling like a king. Each at-bat was a unique, one-of-a-kind experience that could end with so many possibilities. The unpredictability of the moment was what I loved. It is what makes baseball great. Attempting to outthink the pitcher in a game of mental chess is truly one of life's greatest individual rivalries.

Then there was the ride or walk home. Whether I was

crawling into the back seat of my parents' old station wagon or walking the two blocks home in my final several years, it was always with a sense of accomplishment. Win or lose made no difference in retrospect; it was the dirt and sweat on my uniform that left me a proud warrior; the aches that reverberated through my body and mind that have stood the test of time in my memory. I doubt there is a greater first true love.

I still have that old ball glove that served as my sentry during my last seven seasons. It is almost three decades old and still in superb shape. I use it when I have a game of catch with my boys, who are slowly starting to catch the bug. When their hands are large enough, that glove will be passed down to them, along with the wisdom I learned from the game.

THE CRAB APPLE WARS

The Crab Apple Wars were the highlight of every summer during my middle school years. My father worked first shift as an electrician for General Motors, leaving long before we woke up in the morning and not coming home until after three in the afternoon. Mom was an administrative assistant at the hospital and left for work around eight AM, returning home near dinnertime. During the school year, this system worked well. But come the summer, Frank was left in charge of our well-being while Mom and Dad worked to make ends meet. Our first summer home together, I was in sixth grade, Frank was in seventh grade, and our younger brother Jesse had just finished his first-grade year. We lived in a respectable double cul-de-sac with numerous other children our age at home for the summer, and there were a few stay-at-home moms in the neighborhood we could solicit for help in case of an emergency.

Although my brothers and I had a Catholic upbringing, our behavior was the furthest thing possible from saint-like, especially when left with long hours to fill and questionable supervision. Our neighbor directly to our right had a massive backyard that was walled at the far end by a line of thirty-foot pine trees, which blocked out the sight of the car dealership the next street over. The dealership owned a small field behind their lot, which was adjacent to some woods where we had built a tree house that served as our base of operations whenever we played war over the long summer hours.

My father had built the tree house with the understanding that we were to play in the front part of the woods and immediately report any strange individuals that we may encounter out there. Every now and then we would run into a vagrant or two, usually older men, down on their luck and just looking for a shady place to drink their suds. We rarely bothered one another—I can only recall one instance in which we felt uncomfortable enough to even leave the comfort of our fort. We spent our time in the tree house engaging in the usual activities, most of which revolved around some variation of combat. Frank, naturally, was the ringleader, foreshadowing what would become a lifelong military career later on down the line. Sometimes, it was just the three of us, but sometimes we would be joined by a larger team of other neighborhood kids—Johnny, Chuckie, Mike, and Brian—for a more complete game of war. Jesse and I always ended up on the same team, because we could never take the game seriously. Between our bright summer clothes, loud trudging through the brush, and constant giggling, we were sitting ducks. Frank, on the other hand, dominated the game regardless of how many people played. He would squeeze his body into a patch of briars to gain the element of surprise and burst out on unsuspecting passerby, rendering him victorious. The crude sound of our toy guns (or, failing that, the man-made sounds of vaguely gun-shaped sticks) was always followed by, "I got you, you're dead!" Only to be contradicted by the other side's counterargument of, "No, I got you first!"

But by far the best games occurred once a week or so, when, depending on how quickly the grass grew in the field behind the car dealership, one unlucky employee would be granted the unenviable task of mowing the empty lot. The dealership had an old riding lawn mower that immediately caught the attention of anyone within a five-block radius when the engine cranked over. For our crew, it was music to our ears, for it provided us with an opportunity to put our combat skills to the test against a worthy opponent.

Frank, the general, quickly devised a plan of action depending on how many soldiers were in his battalion on the given day. The plan always called for the division of troops, which gave us the advantage of a multiple-front offensive that would bewilder our enemy and make it extremely difficult to offer a counterattack. Additionally, the divided front made it equally difficult for our enemy to give pursuit to his assailants, especially since we knew every fox and rabbit trail in and out of the field. We always had a rendezvous point picked at the beginning of each battle in case things turned ugly. Our general always thought of everything, which was a major asset to our otherwise ignorant army. The final instruction was always the same: wait until the general fires the first shot, before we unleash our wrath.

Our first priority was to gather enough ammunition to withstand a lengthy battle. The field sported a gigantic crab apple tree that supplied us with the necessary arsenal. We would quickly scurry behind the cover of the tall pines to the huge tree, gathering as many crab apples as we could carry in the fronts of our shirts. Thus armed, we would then spread out under the cover of the pines and shrubs that bordered the field, awaiting the initial shot. Frank always had pin-point accuracy, and more often than not the initial shot was a direct hit to the riding mower, if not the rider himself. Once the first shot was fired, all hell broke loose as we bombarded the lawnmower and driver from every direction. An aerial view of the field would have offered a terrifying image as dozens of crab apples painted the sky a reddish-green. It usually took only a few minutes for the rider to either retreat behind the bulk of the mower, or else to turn tail and flee helplessly for the cover of the car lot, abandoning the mower in hopes of surviving the onslaught.

Most of the time, the dealership staff were pretty good sports about the ambush—some would even return fire. They usually waited us out for an hour or so before returning to cut the grass, by which point we'd had our fun and would let them get on with it. I mean, we used the field for baseball and football games all the time. It was adjacent to our tree fort, so it wasn't like it was a huge mystery as to which neighborhood kids were responsible for attacking their employees.

Only once did the war get out of hand, when the rider of the lawn mower was pegged one too many times and recruited some of his coworkers to chase us into the neighborhood. I was terrified, even though we knew the streets like the backs of our hands. We led them on a wild goose chase through several blocks and the surrounding woods before ducking into the sliding glass basement door of Chuckie's house. Chuckie's mom was usually home, but often ran errands during the day, leaving Chuckie a note on the counter letting him know her whereabouts and when she would return. Thankfully, she wasn't home during the chase. We quickly pulled the glass door shut, locked it, and watched behind drawn curtains as the workers ran through the backyard moments later. My brothers and I hid in Chuckie's basement for several hours before sneaking back through the neighborhood to our own house.

Frank was not always the kindest soul to Jesse and me, but I will always remember how protective he was of us during those summers we spent free of our parents' supervision. He gave us enough room to be who we wanted to be, but he made sure at the end of each day that we were still around when our parents arrived home from work. For that and many reasons, I will forever be grateful to him.

BROKEBACK RODEO

Around the time Frank entered high school, the miracle of puberty reared its head for the first time in our household. Frank became excessively moody and withdrawn from family conversations, especially at dinner, and spent the majority of his time at home locked in his room with AC/DC playing loud enough for the whole neighborhood to learn the lyrics. The change caught Jesse and me off guard, as our brother became suddenly estranged from us. Where once Frank was always game for a bit of mooning, or a wedgie, or a sword fight over the old porcelain bowl, now he wanted nothing to do with our juvenile antics.

Baffled, Jesse and I began to spy on Frank whenever possible. If we couldn't be a part of our older brother's new world, than we sure as hell were going to find out what we were missing. Our efforts mainly revolved around two primary locations in the house: Frank's bedroom, and the basement. Unfortunately, we were granted limited access to both when Frank occupied them. We knew there was some serious business going down behind his closed bedroom door, so we did our best to lie down in the hall outside and look under the sliver of space between the bottom of the door and the carpeted entryway. Unfortunately, it was above our capabilities to lie still and quiet long enough to get a decent look. Combine that with the perpetual laughing, and it was no wonder that more often than not Frank quickly opened his door and attempted to squash us like roaches before we could scurry away.

The other hotspot for our spying operation was the basement

steps, which led down to Frank's weight room. It was quite the elaborate setup, especially for a high school freshman. He was extremely strong for his age, and very dedicated to his workout routine, which generally took up several hours of the day. Frank's buddies would come over and lift with him from time to time, always to the steady sounds of Metallica or AC/DC pounding from the boombox.

Once again, Jesse and I did our best to sneak down the creaky wooden stairs while the music blared and the dumbbells clanked, but the giggles, always the giggles did us in, especially when we caught Frank in a muscle pose-off in the basement mirror. Usually there was no one else down there with him, but he would give that mirror all it could take until the moment he heard us on the steps. Then, the mad scramble commenced to get our asses up to the first floor, through the front hallway, and up to my bedroom where we could lock the door. We would sit against the outside wall of my closet and prop our feet against the bedroom door as Frank crashed furiously against it like a battering ram.

On most occasions, we were able to hold off the attack, but I'll be damned if my door frame didn't take a beating. Jesse and I did our best to antagonize Frank, and to his credit, he always did his best to react to our invitations. During one of my recon missions, I observed that Frank had taken a keen interest in showering in our parents' bathroom. In fairness, our parents' shower, with its sliding glass doors and working air vent, was definitely nicer than the drafty one on the second floor that we shared.

Frank was meticulous in his bathing routine. He would walk downstairs with his toiletry kit in hand, in a fluffy purple robe and slippers to boot. I, on the other hand, would turn the shower on, run to my bedroom, strip off my clothes, and run naked back down the hall to jump under the warm water.

I soon decided upon a sinister, possibly even evil plan to

interrupt my older brother's precious shower time. Call it pay-back for the times Frank had pinned me down and dangled a disgusting lugie inches from my face. My mother had a dual sliding glass mirror opposite the entry to her bathroom, and an adjacent vanity where she applied her makeup in the morning. With any plan that requires the element of surprise, the hiding spot is the crucial element that will make or break the success of the mission. Clutching an old leather belt from the hook in my closet, I wedged myself below the vanity counter behind the open bathroom door, undetectable under a pile of my mother's clothes. Victory would be mine this day.

My plan was simply to wait until the end of my broth-er's shower and, upon his exit from the bathroom, to mount upon his back, casting my belt over his head in an attempt to tame the wild bronco. I knew his sheer strength was enough to send me flying, so the ultimate success of my plan relied heav-ily on timing and attention to detail. As I lay beneath the pile of clothes, I listened restlessly to the beating of my heart and unsteadiness of my breath. I closed my eyes and thought about all of the dedicated soldiers in history and the thoughts that must have raced through their minds in the moments before entering battle. Was this to be my moment of unparalleled tri-umph, or yet another disastrous defeat at the hands of my older brother? At that moment, only God knew what awaited in my future. I only wish he would have given me a glimmer of insight into the events that were to follow.

I crouched as patient and stealthy as a mountain lion, wait-ing to pounce as the bathroom door slowly opened and my brother emerged amidst a cloud of steam wearing his vintage purple bathrobe. As Frank walked away from the bathroom door, I sprang into action with a bloodcurdling rebel yell. I bounded onto his back, flinging the belt over his head in an attempt to gain control of the beast as he cried out in utter sur-prise and bucked like a mechanical bull in a biker bar. I held on, wrapping my arms around his neck and sinking my teeth into the flesh of his shoulder. Frank flailed uncontrollably, both of us laughing hysterically yet neither relenting.

My brother's strength was superlative to mine, and I knew it was only a matter of time before my luck ran out. He viciously slammed me onto our parents' bed with a resounding back-body drop, yet somehow I managed to hold on using my legs like a wrestler. Frank spun me round and round, trying to break free from my death lock. Then, in the blink of an eye, the unimaginable happened, and our fates took a sudden, drastic turn for the worse. With tremendous force, Frank slammed me into our parents' bedroom wall, breaking my grip and leaving my entire back and head embedded in the drywall. I remember falling to the carpet covered in plaster dust and looking back at the wall in sheer horror. The hole was roughly two feet in length and almost the same distance in width. It was a massive crater and I knew we were in trouble.

I watched my brother slam his head down repeatedly on our parents' bed, yelling and cursing our fate, because he knew as well as I did that our actions would warrant a serious whooping. I tried to no avail to calm his fears as I continued to stare at the hole in disbelief. I promised that I would assume the brunt of the responsibility, but that would fall on deaf ears once my father viewed the gaping hole next to his bed. Jesse and Dad were out at the store, and Mom was at work, so she wouldn't be around to save us. We knew we had less than an hour left to live. Try as I might, I could think of no way out of this dilemma except to stand and face the music.

When Dad arrived home, we attempted to take the proactive route, cutting him off at the bottom of the stairs to plead our case. I saw his face go white and then red as he bounded up the stairs two at a time. As soon as Dad turned the corner into his bedroom, the yelling and profanity began. He stepped out of his doorway with a wild look in his eyes. I was too terrified by the stupidity of our actions to even listen to the words spewing from his mouth. He was on us in seconds as we struggled to escape his grasp. Luckily, I was able to scoot under his arm, though I still caught a little pop to my backside as I scurried to my bedroom. I locked the door, cowering in my bed as I listened to my dad unleash another string of profanities. In retrospect, and as a father now myself, I would have been equally pissed if my own boys pulled something like this. Frank managed to find refuge in his room as well, while Jesse listened to the action above from the safety of the kitchen. We never really got a word of explanation in, but that probably worked out in our favor. We stayed locked away for the remainder of the day, only daring to poke our heads out from our rooms after Mom came home from work.

Needless to say, once our mother finally managed to calm Dad down, we were grounded for a week. Frank and I uttered not a word to our father for the next week and did our best to avoid him. It took him several nights after work to complete the drywall repairs. Fortunately, my father had the amazing ability to fix just about anything a house full of teenage boys could destroy. Looking back, I guess my plan of attack had a few flaws.

POPS

My father once described himself as a table in a world full of chairs. I wasn't sure what that was supposed to mean, but I didn't have to ponder for long because, true to his nature, he was quick to elaborate. He went into great detail about the differences between tables and chairs. How each plays a significant role and has a defined purpose. Knowing Pops the way I do now, it was his tap dance about how "this is me," and how he's always going to be the way he is. My father has always been the sort of man who does things his own way for his own reasons. It has taken me nearly all of my forty years of life to understand how his experiences and background have shaped him into the most complex individual I have ever met. Initially, I nodded along as I listened to his in-depth analysis of mankind-as-furniture. Given the platform and the time, I'm sure he could have further broken humanity down into subcategories—coffee tables versus formal dining tables; love seats versus settees.

Simply stated, my father is a genius.

I could come up with half a dozen stories about my father's technical prowess off the top of my head, but there's one in particular that has stayed with me for over thirty years. One Sunday, when I was about ten, my fathered borrowed my uncle's mini-van to drive an hour or so down to the Amish community in Central Ohio to pick up a wooden rocking glider. Accompanying him were me, my mother, and my younger brother Jesse. We were nearing our destination when a problem occurred with the steering column. I'm not sure what happened or how, but the result was that my father found himself faced with the daunting task of driving a vehicle that could no longer turn.

Miraculously, he was able to haul the wheel around just enough to turn into a corner gas station, where he found a pay-phone to call my uncle. My uncle left immediately, borrowing our car to come pick us up, be we knew he was well over an hour away. Now, any normal person would have paid to have the mini-van towed backed to Cleveland to be fixed by a certified mechanic and settled in to wait on their ride. But my father was not going to waste an hour of his life sitting around. So, he did what he always did and started tinkering. The high school kid working the register was kind enough to lend him the gas station's tool box while we waited and that was all the encouragement my pops needed.

All I saw of my father for the next hour was his hand whenever he reached out from under the car and asked my mother or the fascinated cashier for a tool. Somehow, to this day I don't know how, he finally managed to rig the steering system with the sort of coated cording one might use for hanging laundry. He was just finishing up when my uncle pulled into the gas station like a bat out of hell. My dad emerged to explain whatever magic he'd worked.

My uncle ended up driving the mini-van all the way back to Cleveland, while my father, mother, brother, and I followed him in our car. The van made it all the way home without a hiccup.

My father was and still is a man who loves hard, believes in strong discipline, and would give his life for his family at a moment's notice. I won't say that I always agreed with the way he and my mother handled our family's issues, but as a husband and father now myself, I've made my peace with much of what I used to resent.

Dealing with similar challenges in raising my own boys to what Pops faced with us, I've learned to appreciate that although his love was tough at times, it was unconditional. I hope my boys will someday feel that way about me. I want them to know that they can always count on me, the way I could always count on my dad.

My dad never gave up on me, even when I presented him with some extremely challenging moments. He's saved my behind more times than I can count, and still would even to this day. There were many periods of our lives when we didn't see eye to eye. Hell, there were significant periods of times when we didn't even speak, but I always knew he was only a phone call away. I have never doubted his love for our family, especially me. He can be a stubborn pain in the ass sometimes, but I am proud now to say that I am certain I have inherited that trait from him.

Parenthood is nothing more than a test of patience. Some days my best shines through, and others, well, not so much. Yet, I think the bonding love that exists between my father and me is also alive and present in the relationship that I have with my own sons. I am my father in so many ways, and for that I am truly grateful. I might not always agree with him, but I have tremendous respect and admiration for his inner courage. I guess I, like him, am another table in a world full of chairs. And I have no doubt in my mind that my pops did it right!

A RETURN TO CATHOLICISM

It was toward the latter end of my freshman year that I made the difficult decision to leave my public high school and return to parochial education. My parents were less than thrilled by the notion, primarily due to the costs of Catholic school. Matters weren't helped by the fact that I had difficulty explaining to them why I wanted to transfer out in the first place. My grades were solid, I'd made a few friends, and I was even on the freshman baseball team, having managed some nice plays on balls hit by the varsity coach in my tryout.

True enough, during my freshman year, I had maintained a few close friendships with Big Red and some of my lunchroom buddies from eighth grade, and it helped that my brother was a pretty well-known sophomore, which lent me some credibility among the upper grades. Still, by no stretch of the imagination was I what one might call "popular" with the rest of my class. I spent the majority of my freshman year ducking into classes right on time and otherwise keeping my head down so as to avoid the attention of my personal demons, who had unfortunately followed me from middle school. A small group of peers in my eighth-grade class had latched onto my squirrelly sitting ritual early the previous year, and now I was stuck with at least one of these lovely individuals in every period. None of them had yet tired of taking every possible opportunity to point out my oddities to anyone who cared to listen. Thankfully, none of my dedicated tormentors were exactly popular in their own right, and most of my other classmates couldn't have cared less about my peculiar tic. Still, the targeting itself was enough to send my anxiety through the roof and decimate my self-esteem.

Freshman year, I had minimal social life outside the confines of school. Most Friday nights, while others were going out to football or basketball games, I could be found at home watching a movie or hanging out with Jesse. Best case scenario was when our high school football team was playing away, and Big Red and some of the old lunch box gang would gather at one of our houses to shoot pool. On those nights, we would walk the neighborhoods, eventually ending up in the bottom of the park to smoke some cigarettes that someone had banked from their parents. Life on the home front stayed fairly consistent to the previous year or so. My parents had their ups and downs, but somewhere in the back of my mind, I was certain that sooner or later they would find a way to resolve their issues.

Red and I continued to develop our friendship, even though it got a little weird when his older sister decided to date Frank for a few months. We continued with our weekend sleepovers, though not with quite the regularity we'd maintained over the summer months. We would wait until everyone fell asleep before sneaking out of the sliding glass back door and down to the park to raise a little mischief. We almost always got caught the following morning because our shoes were muddy, or we left the back door unlocked. But Red's mom, who was always disappointed in our antics, still found a level of humor in our mediocre truancy. So, all things considered, I suppose things couldn't have looked bad to an outside observer. But the truth of the matter was that my ship was sinking deeper by the day. The anxiety of dealing with the daily targeting was exhausting, and if that wasn't enough, the uncertainty at home left me with no reprieve outside of school. My mind was screaming for a change, and I wanted to walk on to somewhere I could find a new start.

So as freshman year was winding down, I grew more

adamant than ever about switching schools for my sophomore year. I remember my parents and Frank trying to rationalize my decision, yet they never could quite get it. Why would I want to leave a school that I could walk to? I was not required to wear a uniform, there were plenty of girls, and best of all, it was free. Instead, I chose a forty-five-minute bus ride, a uniform, an all-male school, and a return to daily religious studies.

"Yes," was all I could muster. But then again, my parents had no idea the hurt and torment that had been running through my head over the past year. They knew from our conversations that there were a few kids who were mean to me, but I don't think any of them knew how frequent the torment was, or how strongly it affected me, and there was no way I would ever have admitted to them how their deteriorating relationship added to my strain. They had enough going on in their lives, I thought, without having to deal with my problems.

After that, I left my house promptly at six-thirty every morning to walk to the public bus stop two blocks away. Most days I made it in ten minutes, but I was so worried about missing the bus that I wasn't taking any chances. The bus was filled primarily with other boys heading to my high school. I was fortunate that one of the more well-liked sophomore students on the bus played on my summer league baseball team, so it helped with the anxiety of being relatively unknown.

I hated taking the bus, but what worried me most was the chance of missing the afternoon ride home. The bus picked us up in the school's back parking lot, but it left on schedule regardless of who was left behind. I lived a long way from my high school, so missing the afternoon bus meant a lengthy afternoon of dull waits in sketchy Cleveland bus stations to make the multiple transfers back to my own neighborhood. I told not a soul at my new school about my home life, or the persistent torment I had gone through the last two years. I was a world away from my past, and that was what I wanted.

The unfortunate part of choosing to transfer schools was that I began to see less and less of Big Red. I had yet to make new friends worth spending time with outside of school, so my Friday nights were still quiet. By that point in the week, I had logged enough miles on public transportation that all I truly wanted was to relax before the grind began again. Then, in the spring of my sophomore year, Red was cut from the JV baseball team despite an amazing tryout. It really set him off, and most of the other guys on the team agreed that Red had been given the short end of the stick.

This ended up being the final straw for Red. His family's transition to Cleveland from central Ohio had not been a smooth one, and he never really felt like he belonged, struggling to fit into a new school while miserable over the loss of his old friends. I think baseball was the only thing that had made his life in Cleveland bearable. That weekend, Red proceeded to pack up his life and moved back to live with his extended family in central Ohio for the remainder of his high school years. I think it was difficult for Red's family to see him go, but they understood that he needed to get back to where he belonged. He moved in with his uncle, aunt, and two young cousins, and played on the varsity baseball team that spring. The next few times I saw him, Red smiled more than he had in all the time I'd known him, and I was happy for it. We stayed in contact with weekly phone calls, and I'd still drop by his house and have dinner with his mom and sisters. I even had a few opportunities to go watch Red play football and baseball over the next two years.

I knew now more than ever that I was going to be a lonely soul throughout the duration of my high school experience. Not only was my sole compadre gone, but also my escape when I needed to get away from home for a minute. Never did I think Red would actually leave and head back to his old stomping grounds. As long as his family was here, I'd thought for certain he would be around. Fortunately, Frank took pity on me the weekend Red left and invited me to tag along to a party he was going to. There was a girl named Aubrey in his junior class who really liked him, and she'd invited him to a birthday gathering at her house. I knew he really had no interest in Aubrey outside of being her friend, so I have to wonder if he attended the party just to get me out of the house.

It was at this party that I first met Bumps. She became the first real love of my life, and I spent that night and most of the next year and a half in her company. So as fortune would have it, I lost my best friend and found my first love in the space of one weekend. I was instantly drawn to everything about Bumps. We spent the party dancing and talking about music. In addition to being unbelievably beautiful, she had a spirit and soul to match. I promised her at the end of the party that I would come visit her at the independent grocery store where she worked the following day. Truth be told, I had no way to get there except to walk, but I'll be damned if I didn't, two miles each way. A round trip of four miles for a five-minute conversation, and it was worth every moment. We became a couple in short order.

Bumps was a year ahead of me in school, had her driver's license and even her own car. I, on the other hand, was fifteen with no license or car. Yet for whatever reason, none of that ever really mattered. She wanted to be a marine biologist and I never doubted for a second that she would be. For her birthday, I bought her tickets to Sea World, which was about an hour away from us. The girl loved Shamu and all the splendor that the ocean could offer. She drove, and we held hands the entire way. Watching the smile on her face was unforgettable. Bumps was genuine, hysterical, and sincerely cared about my well-being. It was refreshing. When we were together, nothing else in the world mattered to me. The fact that we attended different schools made weekends a new and wonderful endeavor. Was it perfect? No. What high school relationship isn't subject to the twists and turns of that tumultuous age? However, the one certainty was that together, we danced like no one else. Our time together was full of sunsets over Lake Erie, drive-in movies, shooting pool while dropping quarters in the jukebox, or just holding hands as we drove around for hours listening to music. Bumps had an ear for music and we wore out every mix tape she made that spring and summer. I was ten feet tall when I was with Bumps, and I was the envy of all the fellas my age. My parents absolutely adored her, and they greatly appreciated all the positive support and love she gave me during that difficult time in my life.

Except for my parents, she was the only individual that I could have truly meaningful conversations with, and that was something I definitely needed. Bumps taught me the importance of being a positive person and being confident in who I am. Unfortunately, she saw a great deal of the ugliness of my life at home, but she did all she could to take me away from that scene, if only for a few hours on Friday or Saturday night. She never judged either of my parents, only offered support by way of looking out for their son. Twenty-five years later, I still chuckle at how Bumps got her nickname, but I'll never tell. That is a story that will forever be shared only between us. The fairy tale ended when Bumps went away to college and I started my senior year of high school. I held onto my feelings for her far too long after it was over. It was painful, certainly, but I would come to appreciate the experience for all it taught me about the depth and scope of a first love lost.

TO SAVE IT ALL

It was a trip to save it all, although we had no idea that was the purpose of it until years later. In late October of my junior year, my parents went all-in to salvage the shattered remains of their marriage with a romantic trip to Mexico, making the ill-fated decision to leave Frank in charge while they were away. Frank and I were old enough to be left at home with our studies and our part-time jobs. Jesse was to stay with us after school until dinner, at which time he was to pack his bag and cross the cul-de-sac to sleep at the neighbors' house. The neighbors had two boys close to his age, and they would also be keeping a vigilant eye on Frank and me from across the way.

Nonetheless, the night before his departure, my father pulled Frank and me aside and issued a stern decree to be on our best behavior. We were instructed to go to school and to our jobs, and without a doubt, there was to be no funny business whatsoever.

Friday afternoon, Frank dropped off my parents at the airport for their last shot at finding happiness. A few hours later, he opened the front door to what must have been half the public high school. Cars were packed bumper to fender around both cul-de-sacs and all the way up the street. Within the first hour of the party, all three floors of our house were jam-packed with high school students. I personally was not that interested in drinking during this lavish Friday-night bash for two reasons: first, I had recently failed the maneuverability portion of my driver's examination, and therefore still couldn't drive a car; and second, my relationship with Bumps had veered off course and we had recently broken up.

As bad as breakups are regardless of the circumstances, a broken heart in high school is its own unique brand of hell. The close quarters combined with turbulent hormones creates an intensely public scene. Everyone knows that you and your previous significant other are no longer an item, so every male vulture is on high alert. Lifelong friendships are tested and shattered in the span of a weekend hookup. To add insult to injury, Bumps was, in all honesty, well out of my league, so while other guys positioned themselves to make a move on her, the line waiting for the opportunity to date me was essentially nonexistent. We had been going out for about six months at that point, and I had been in a foul mood for the better part of a month when Bumps finally had enough. Sure enough, potential suitors lined up the moment news of the break-up hit the hallways.

I walked into the backyard in an attempt to clear my head, just in time to see two boys sharing a joint get the life scared out of them by a skunk that waddled out of the woods. Chuckling to myself, I sat down on the deck of the pool as I listened to the party inside grow in excitement. My thoughts soon drifted to my parents and their most recent struggles. Although I didn't know at the time the exact purpose of their trip to Mexico, I had an inkling that the time alone together would likely change things, be it for better or worse.

The party lasted a mere two hours before the neighbor across the street showed up at the door and informed Frank that everyone must leave immediately. Within a few minutes, two police cruisers pulled into the driveway, which expedited the disbursement process considerably. People rushed out the back door of our house, stumbling into the dark as they jumped the fence and scrambled in all different directions, determined not to get arrested for underage drinking. The neighbor, who assumed responsibility for the disastrous scene at hand, was our saving grace.

Frank's party, which he had planned from the moment he learned my parents were leaving the country, was over. He and his merry band of adolescent miscreants had exercised every ounce of their creative genius to stockpile cases of beer and liquor in preparation of the festivities, most of it spirited away from the grocery store where Frank worked inside large detergent boxes. In the end, their months of diligent effort were all in vain.

Eventually, there were only two people left, not counting the few stragglers hiding out in the neighbors' yards waiting for the cops to clear out: Angelina, a sophomore friend of Frank's, and some freshman we found vomiting in Jesse's closet. Frank asked me to take his car and drive Angelina home while he dealt with the drunk kid. I reluctantly agreed, even though I was fully aware of the potential consequences. Taking a few deep breaths, I glanced over at Angelina and turned over the ignition. A cold rain was just beginning to fall as I backed the 1984 Dodge Charger out of the driveway. I had only driven at night a few times before, and never in the rain, but I was fairly confident in my abilities on the road. It was just the damn cones on the Driver's Ed course that I couldn't get a grasp on. We had traveled a few miles from home, mainly on back roads, and I was beginning to breathe a little easier, when I missed a turn and was forced up to a busy intersection. The last thing I remember is turning left at the light.

When life slowly came back into focus, my knees were embedded in the lower dashboard on either side of the steering wheel. Angelina had hit her head on the windshield, but thankfully had been wearing her seatbelt. I pried my knees from the dash and attempted to crawl out of the remains of my brother's Charger. I knew the police would be arriving any moment—we had crashed right in front of the station.

I stumbled over to the BMW that I had smashed into and watched an older gentleman and a frazzled golden retriever crawl out of the mangled driver's side door. Ears ringing, I asked him frantically for a quarter to make a phone call. Equally dazed, he automatically reached into his pocket to hand me a few coins. I took the change and bolted to the pay phone at the corner of the intersection to dial my neighbor's phone number with shaking fingers. He barely managed to get out the greeting before I was screaming into the phone that I'd been in an accident. I'm positive this guy was regretting the moment he ever agreed to keep an eye on us while my parents were in Mexico. The next thirty minutes was a blur of police and tow car lights. The police officer berated me repeatedly for driving with just a permit, although thankfully Angelina had her license, so I wasn't in as much trouble as I otherwise would have been. Angelina was stable enough to answer questions about the accident, but was suffering from a terrible headache. She refused to go in the ambulance though, preferring to wait for her parents to come pick her up and take her to the hospital. I held Angelina's hand and helped her into the back seat of her parent's car when they arrived. We spoke the next day and Angelina confirmed that she had a concussion.

I watched as my brother's Charger and the BMW were dragged from the scene by two different wreckers. The poor guy I'd smashed into—and his dog—were visibly shaken. I felt terrible about the entire situation. I apologized profusely and learned that he was the owner of the local video store where my family rented our movies. The police released me to the custody of my neighbor and cited me with failure to yield to oncoming traffic. The officer shook his head as he handed me my ticket, and my neighbor drove me home without uttering a word. I trudged past the totaled Charger, which had been towed back to our house. Another brilliant idea on our part. Who tows a wrecked five-hundred-dollar car back to their house? It sat there all week till our parents got home, leaking oil down the driveway.

I found Frank sitting at the kitchen table in a stupor, shaking his head in disbelief. As angry as he was about his car, he was actually more concerned for my well-being as he told me the story of the freshman in Jesse's closet. He had urinated all over himself and was sitting in his underwear when Frank found him. I chuckled at the story, but in the back of my mind I knew hell was coming. Our parents were going to kill us. Unfortunately, we still had an entire school week ahead of us to think about the stupidity of the night's events before they would return from Mexico. In this moment, we did what any troubled youth might do when facing the damnation of his parents: we called Grandma and pleaded with her to stay with us for the remainder of the week.

The arrival of Grandma on the scene brought a calming influence to the chaotic atmosphere. The totaled Charger sat in the driveway and served as a constant visual reminder of our foolishness. Gossip spread through our neighborhood like the plague. I was curious what my neighbors were saying about us in the confines of their homes. Frank spent every evening for the remainder of the week sitting at the kitchen table, sipping his cache of beers and counting down the hours to our demise. I spent the next few days home from school, recovering from my physical and emotional wounds. Jesse came home from the neighbors' and provided us with constant reminders as to how much trouble we were going to be in, for which we thanked him caustically.

Friday afternoon found Frank dropping me off at work in our parents' car, on his way to pick them up from the airport. As I got out of the car, we both looked at each other as if it might be the last time we would see each other in this lifetime. I have never prayed for a shift in the produce department to last longer than I did that day. Frank was to pick up our parents at the airport, and then they were going to drop him off at his job. My father was then going to pick us both up from work at ten that evening. I watched the minutes tick by into hours. By nine, I had broken out in a cold sweat. I only had a few hours left on this earth and there was so much I had left to discover. What was to become of Frank and me?

Frank's workplace was further away from our home than mine, so naturally my father picked him up first. I could see Frank cowering in the back seat of the Chevy Lumina when it roared to a stop outside the grocery store. He had clearly already endured ten minutes of hell, and I could tell he had been crying. My father leapt out of the driver's side with the ferocity of a lion and instructed me to get into the car. I had seen my father angry before, but nothing could ever have paralleled the rage in his voice that night. I dove for cover into Frank's waiting arms and together we sat trembling behind the driver's seat in hopes of avoiding our father's outstretched arm.

It was the longest five miles of our lives. Dad was pissed, and he let us know it. He kept hitting the brakes to turn around to yell at us. I was certain that we were going to die. In my father's defense, he had every right to be as irate as he was in that moment. Now that I am a father myself, I can only imagine how angry I would be if I had to return to the country after attempting to save my marriage only to be betrayed by my two oldest sons' adolescent hijinks. My father always put a lot of trust in us, much the same way I trust my own boys. Yes, he was angry, but I can imagine that it was mainly out of fear of what could have happened to us. We were lucky that the outcome was not more horrific than a totaled Dodge Charger. Even at the time, I couldn't hold his anger against him. As we inched closer to our house, a light snow began cascading from the clouds. It was the first snowfall of the year and I was certain it would be my last. Frank and I knew that hell was to be paid the moment we pulled into the driveway. Unfortunately,

Frank was going to receive the majority of it. We clung to one another, paralyzed with fear.

As the Lumina bellowed into the driveway, past the destroyed Charger, I knew my life on earth was about to end. The second the Lumina rolled to a halt, Frank and my dad both jumped out and started circling the car. The dance had begun. Dad had superior reach, but Frank had speed on his side, enabling him to dodge and weave between our father's snatching arms. They were soon joined by my mother, who came running out of the garage to try and calm my father down. All but forgotten, I unfolded carefully from the back seat of the Lumina and stood by watching, at a loss as to what to do. All the while, the snow continued to fall peacefully on the four of us. It was a surreal moment. Suddenly, Frank made a break for it. With the speed of a gazelle, he bolted across the neighbor's yard through the sticking snow, making for the woods. Frank knew every remote trail and hiding spot there was to find out there, and I knew in an instant that Dad would never catch him if he made it into the cover of the trees.

I stood by in disbelief as my mother cried. I don't know how long we both stood there, but it felt like an eternity. There was so much I wanted to say to her. I wanted Mom to know how sorry I was that Frank and I had let them down. Yet, I never said a word. To our astonishment, my father did return, covered in a light dusting of snow, without my brother. I was worried that his wrath would now fall on me, as I was technically the one who had wrecked the car, but instead he just sent me to my room. I lay on my bed in bewilderment as I listened to my parents quarreling downstairs over his handling of the situation. My mother was hysterical with worry, as Frank had run into the woods in only his short-sleeved work shirt. The snow was still falling steadily, and she was adamant that my father go back out there to find Frank. We all knew Frank wasn't staying in the woods. He'd only done that to lose our father. I figured he would eventually make his way to one of his friend's houses. When I heard the garage door open, I got up off my bed and peered through the blinds of my bedroom window. My father was inching the Lumina out of the driveway and into the snow-covered street. He was going to try and find his boy. My mother opened my door, crumpled tissue in hand, mascara streaked down her face with tears. She wasn't angry. She was terrified. It broke my heart. One simple question was all she asked: "What the hell happened here last week?" All I could do was hang my head. I'll never forget the hurt in her eyes as she quietly pulled my door closed.

An hour had passed before the Lumina came struggling back up the driveway, which was now slippery with at least three inches of early November snow. I watched as my father exited the car, again without Frank. There was a minute or two before I heard the garage door close. I imagined Dad standing in the garage, trying to wrap his head around this whole catastrophic situation. At this point, anger had surrendered to disappointment. He was calmer now, softly reassuring my mother that although he hadn't managed to find Frank, he was sure he'd found somewhere safe to hide.

I made my way to the top of the staircase and sat down on the second step from the top, feeling like a little kid. Jesse had been in bed for hours and was oblivious to all that had transpired. Dad described to my mother the route he had pursued in hopes of finding Frank. He had circled the park several blocks away and even stopped over at the house of a friend of Frank's who lived near the park. Mom had been making phone calls to the parents of all of Frank's friends while Dad was out, and together, they had put the word out that he was missing. At this point, all they wanted was to know that Frank was alright.

Every passing minute led to more tears from my mother and a growing anxious frustration from my father. Eventually, a call came in from the mother of Frank's buddy Earl. Frank had made it to their house roughly five miles away, soaked and freezing and visibly upset. My mother took the phone call and agreed that it was best if Frank stayed there for a few days until cooler heads prevailed. My father might not have agreed, but he remained silent. When he returned home a few days later, Frank told me that he'd been lying face down in the snow at the bottom of the park while Dad circled the block calling for him. Sleep eluded me that night, the clenching knots in my stomach keeping me awake. I lay there watching the rise and fall of my chest as I took exaggerated breaths, realizing our actions may have just led to the ultimate demise of my parents' marriage.

The next morning, my father had my brother's Dodge Charger towed to the junkyard. My family was never the same.

THE FALLOUT

Over the next few months, I watched and waited and hoped against all hope that somehow my parents would patch things up and everything would go back to normal. But it just wasn't in the cards, and so we began the difficult transition into life as a divorced family. Frank managed to miss out on all the fun by heading off to college to room with one of his high school buddies. Jesse and I were less fortunate, stuck on the home front and unable to avoid the messy first year of the divorce.

I was a senior in high school, while Jesse was entering eighth grade. The divorce settlement called for us to split time evenly between our parents. In an effort to not upset Jesse more than necessary, my parents allowed him to stay in his current middle school, so I was saddled with the responsibility of driving him to and from school every day. I spent a great deal of my senior year driving Jesse around in an old Pontiac Grand Am with a busted transmission.

In the fallout from the divorce, Jesse and I struggled to build some sense of normalcy in our new lives. We shared rooms at both of our parents' new residences. My father had given us the master suite in his condo and built us lofts, which provided us with a private bathroom and plenty of room to cohabitate in relative peace. At my mother's apartment, Jesse and I slept on bunkbeds that barely fit into the second bedroom. The room's door was actually two sliding doors—the space was initially intended as a study in the apartment's layout. The doors opened to the dining area, and I spent many nights lying on the bottom bunk, listening to my mother cry softly as she shuffled papers trying to figure out how she was going to survive on her current salary.

The divorce left me angry and bitter at just about everything. I hated going back and forth between my parents' houses every week, living out of my suitcase as if I had no home instead of two. I continued to work at the grocery store throughout my senior year, and with the profound support of my produce manager, was able to acquire more hours to help offset the rising costs of my situation. Mario was a middle-aged Italian man with a thick accent, a bald head, and a huge heart. My mother had reached out to him and informed him of the challenges at home, and he did his best to mentor me through a difficult time. He was ever forgiving of my tardiness and call-offs from work, and stood behind me when some in the department expressed dissatisfaction with my attendance. He never revealed my family's secret and continued to support me until the day I handed in my notice a few weeks before graduation.

Eventually, the strain of the back and forth between residences became too much for me, and I decided to live with my mother full-time. The day after announcing my decision, I walked into her apartment to hear my father's voice on the phone. He was upset by my choice, but at that point I really couldn't speak to my dad. I was having difficulty speaking to anyone. I slid my bedroom doors shut and flung myself onto the bottom bunk, curling up and covering my head. I went to sleep wondering if my dad would retaliate by taking my car away.

In the morning, my car was still there. Dad was willing to let me use the car as long as I agreed to pick Jesse up after school and drop him off at the condo during his weeks. I relented, and many days I went to school, picked up Jesse, and delivered him to my father's residence before heading to work. I was seventeen, leaving home at seven in the morning and returning home at ten at night. As a result, my efforts in school were understandably sub-par, but thankfully my teachers were aware of my situation. I only got in trouble at school once during my senior year. The morning my parents finalized their divorce, I broke wind in my history class—not just a muffled noise but a sonic boom that totally derailed the lesson. My history teacher was tough, a football and wrestling coach known for his no-nonsense persona. He instantly dismissed me from class and sent me to see the dean. The dean, an elderly vet who smelled of cigarettes, was of course unimpressed by my behavior. He grumbled about immaturity as he wrote me up, but all I could do was wonder what this old seadog thought he could do to me that was worse than what I was dealing with on a daily basis. Finally, the strain of the past few months reached a boiling point, and I blurted out that he could do what he wanted, frankly, because at that moment my parents were downtown signing away their marriage and I really didn't care.

It was at this precise moment that my head dropped into my hands and I began to sob uncontrollably. At first, I thought the dean would tell me to quit my sniffling and man up. However, I must have melted a layer of ice from that old curmudgeon's heart that day. He simply put down his pen before the ink had dried on my disciplinary write-up and sent me off to wash my face and go back to class with a stern warning. Later that day, I crossed paths with my history teacher. He had spoken with the dean and gotten the low-down. He expressed his sympathies and told me that in the future it would be wiser to deal with my emotional distress by using my voice rather than my rear end. I couldn't help but agree.

The old seadog died a few years later of lung cancer. That incident was my sole interaction with him while attending school there. Twenty years later, that tough old history teacher is still there inspiring and educating young men as they stand on the threshold of adulthood. I learned that sometimes the toughest, most thick-skinned people hide the deepest wells of empathy in their hearts.

A SEASON TO REMEMBER

Senior year is supposed to be a time of optimism and preparation for young adult life and all that lies ahead, but for me, it was a living hell. The only thing that got me through that year was my bond with my little brother.

My father is a jack of all trades. He could and still can fix any maintenance issue a house can throw at him. At that time, I was not nearly as capable, but I still tried my best to assume the role of handyman at my mother's apartment. Thankfully, repairs to the apartment were generally fixed by the maintenance man at the complex. But my mom often needed me in a pinch to step in for my father and help to preserve a sense of family and tradition for Jesse—and for the two of us, I think. Christmas had always been a special time of year for our family, but that first holiday season felt nothing like years past, with the debilitating fog of the divorce having settled over us all. Nevertheless, my mother was determined to keep the holiday spirit alive, and even though we weren't about to trudge off into the woods and to chop down our own tree, she would be damned if we were not going to have something to decorate.

The first Saturday of December, I came home from working the evening shift to find a scraggly Christmas tree out in the parking lot, leaning against my mom's car. I shook my head in disbelief. Clearly, she had realized too late that she would not be able to drag it up three flights of stairs on her own and was hoping Jesse and I would handle it in the morning.

The excitement of the holiday season, and the tree itself, had always started to build in me immediately after Halloween. It still does—I get giddy these days when I see the first Hallmark Christmas movie on TV the first of November. But I had no Christmas spirit that year. The idea of only spending Christmas Eve with Jesse and not seeing my Pops was weighing heavily on my mind. There was no joy that year, only heartache, and I didn't want a sparsely decorated little Charlie Brown tree sitting in the living room to serve as a month-long reminder of how terrible life had become.

As a result, I was less than thrilled at the prospect trying to hoist this tree up three flights of stairs. But my mother was insistent, and I had work at eleven that morning, so I was in no mood to argue. I grabbed the bottom of the tree and told Jesse to take the top. We made it halfway up the first flight before he started struggling. We ended up dragging the tree all the way upstairs, scattering pine needles in our wake. I wouldn't be surprised if some of them are still embedded in the cheap hallway carpeting to this day. We finally managed to shove the tree through the front door and haul it over to the spot our mom had designated in the living room.

In years past it had always been my father's responsibility to put the Christmas tree in the stand, but this year the job fell on me. We had owned the same metal stand since I was little, but after the divorce it must have ended up hidden amongst the boxes in storage, because I have no recollection of ever seeing it again. My mother had instead purchased a plastic stand to hold our Christmas tree. After much jostling, cussing, and a few whacks with a rubber mallet, I miraculously managed to stand the tree upright and tightened the skeletal screws with all my might. Victorious, I finally slid out from under the tree, dusting pine needles off my work shirt as I admired my handiwork. With the tree in position, I was dismayed to see how skinny it looked compared to our family trees of the past. Nevertheless, I offered to finish off this annual task by giving the tree its first drink of water.

My mother carefully handed me a large measuring cup filled with water, which the tree instantly swallowed. I handed the cup back to her several times, with similar results. I couldn't believe how dry this Christmas tree was; I grumbled to my mother that it must have been cut down during the summer. It wasn't until the fourth measuring cup that I realized that the patch of carpet that I had been kneeling on was saturated with water—as were my work pants. I yelled in disgust as I flung the tree over in a herculean fit of rage, only to discover that in my determination to get the tree to stand straight, I had managed to smack a hole in the bottom of the cheap plastic stand.

The carpet was drenched, and my mom frantically ran downstairs to the apartment below us to make sure the water had not seeped through their ceiling. I tore the busted plastic stand from the stump of the Christmas tree, carrying it with me to the dumpster as I ran to my car. I was now late for work and had to drive there in wet khakis. Fortunately, my mother called ahead and spoke to my manager, so when I arrived all he did was chuckle as I broke into my frantic alibi. He waved it off and laughed aloud as he pushed his way through the swinging double doors that led to the back room of the produce department. As I mentioned before, he was simply an amazing individual. By the time I arrived home that night, my mother had replaced the plastic stand with a metal one. Thank goodness. She'd even managed to get the tree standing upright.

What started out as a disaster became a treasured memory for many years to come. Every time I see one of those damn plastic tree stands, I remember that difficult winter and how we made it work. My family never bought another plastic tree stand. Even my own boys know we use metal or nothing.

GRAD THEFT AUTO

Through the powers of divine intervention, I somehow managed to pull my act together academically and finish high school with a respectable grade point average. I was quite proud of myself considering the ongoing stress in my personal life. The new year brought more of the same old challenges, but somehow, I managed to survive to graduation. After two years in the produce game, I finally hung up my apron, eager to begin the next phase of my life and hopeful that a change of scenery and a little independence would help facilitate a new direction for me.

I had been accepted to a well-respected liberal arts college about a half hour away from my parents. Although my grades were alright, there is no way I had the academic marks to get in. However, my senior biology teacher was a part-time professor at the college and wrote me a glowing recommendation. I have no idea why, because I was at best an average student in her class. But although she marked up my biology tests like nobody's business, she was known around school for her selfless acts of kindness. She was a brilliant scientist and displayed a witty sense of humor that went a long way in a classroom full of high school boys.

The best part was that I was going to be reunited with Big Red. He and I and one of his friends from central Ohio would be rooming together. Red and I had stayed in constant contact during senior year, primarily by way of phone calls. I knew he was thinking of applying to the same college, partially because he missed his family and wanted to be a little closer to them.

I was undecided as to what career path I wanted to follow, but I had thought about teaching or studying history. Red was all-in on psychology. The mind and the way it worked fascinated him.

Frank and his girlfriend at the time drove in from college to attend my high school graduation, along with Jesse and my mother. My father and I still weren't on speaking terms, so he didn't make an appearance. The divorce had hurt my father immensely—I knew that even then—and our many discussions over the past twenty years have offered greater insight to his struggles at the time. My mother and his boys meant the world to him. He wanted us to grow up to be respectable men, and although his love was tough at times, there were times when tough love was what we needed. I hold no ill feeling toward Dad for not attending my graduation. That year was taxing on the entire family, and it certainly took its toll on him.

My mother tried her best to make my graduation special even though it was a lousy time in our lives. A crowd of four cheered for me as I strolled across the stage to accept my degree, but the crowning achievement of four years' worth of academic work was admittedly quite anticlimactic. I guess I had built up graduation in my mind as a victorious celebration. The crowd would erupt in cheers when my name was called, and I'd wave emphatically at my family as I glided across the stage into the dean's waiting handshake, and then off I would go into adulthood. The reality felt a lot more like wearing a dress and holding a piece of paper.

After the ceremony we went to my grandparents' house, where the six of us had dinner and a graduation cake. I never had a chance to have a larger party with my extended family and friends, but I was too excited about college and a fresh start to really care. I was determined to put all of the heartache and sleepless nights behind me and start my life over again.

After the party at my grandparents' house ended, my brothers and I returned to Mom's apartment with Frank's girlfriend in tow. We had been home for fifteen minutes when Frank announced that he was going to need to use my car for the weekend.

Before I could formulate a protest, he added that he'd already obtained my father's permission to borrow the car, which, considering that I hadn't really spoken to the man in almost a year, meant squat to me. I was the one who drove that piece of junk to hell and back. I was the one who'd adjusted the front headlight that for some incomprehensible reason had been installed pointing straight skyward. And I was the one who had saved up the money to have the transmission rebuilt after Frank destroyed the original one attempting neutral drops in his senior year.

"Hell no, you can't take my car for the weekend!" I said, indignant, but Frank insisted that his old high school buddies were all back in town on break, and anyway, he didn't want to be stuck at home with his girlfriend, he wanted to be able to take her out while they were here. "No," I said again. I had just graduated. This was supposed to be my big weekend and here he was, trying to take my ride to go out and party.

It doesn't take much in my family for an argument to become a fight, so Frank and I were on the verge of throwing punches within seconds. My mother screamed at us and then, only the good Lord knows why, she called my father. At that point in time, Dad really did not like to be anywhere near Mom, so the arrival of my father on the scene did not calm the hornet's nest that had already been stirred up. Within minutes, my brother, father, and I were all shouting over each other. The car was never put in my name. It still belonged to my pops. I really had no legal leg to stand on. But the fact remained that while Frank was off having a merry time in college, avoiding the fallout from the divorce, I had spent the past year chauffeuring Jesse between school, my parent's homes, and everywhere else in between, all while driving that old jalopy to work and back several nights a week to help my mom put food on the table. And now, on my graduation weekend, Frank wanted to take my car to hang out with his buddies and Dad was just going to let him? Seeing red, I voiced my discontent for all to hear.

As the fight escalated, Mom started getting frightened, so I left abruptly to take a walk and cool off. After several minutes of venting my frustrations to the evening air I returned home, only to find all the stuff that I kept in my car sitting in a heap in my now empty parking space. That shit stole my car. I laughed initially at the thought of Frank driving away in my car. I can't believe that shit stole my car. I kept repeating that to myself as I paced around the parking lot for the better part of ten minutes, before I suddenly just plopped down in my empty parking space and cried. In utter shock and disbelief, it all came pouring out of me. I never drove that car again. Frank took it back to college with him and I lost my wheels.

Well, I thought to myself, this was going to throw a wrench in my summer plans. I was scheduled to leave on a senior trip with Big Red and his friends from central Ohio the next day for a week-long celebration in the Smoky Mountains of Tennessee, and afterward I was supposed to begin my summer job landscaping for an acquaintance of my mother's.

While I was away on my trip, Mom purchased me a new mountain bike to ride the seven miles each way to and from work. I had to leave an hour before my shift started and often didn't arrive home until six or seven in the evening, but I was able to save a lot of money that summer and was in the best shape of my life by the time classes started. I used the money I made landscaping to purchase a 1988 GMC Sonoma truck, an old manual five-speed clunker that had over a hundred-thousand miles on her. It was my first truck and I intended to drive that beauty until the day she died.

I will always remember the love and support my mother gave me my senior year of high school. I was a hot mess, emotionally speaking, and she helped me find the solutions to all my conflicts. Most of all, she taught me how to stand back up when life knocks you down.

LEARNING MY WAY

There I stood, shoulder to shoulder with Big Red, waving goodbye to our mothers as they pulled away and left us standing on the lawn of our first college dorm. We were only a thirty-minute drive from my mother's home, and I was excited to be reunited with my old friends, among them Red, our buddy Beef, and a guy named Scooter. My college experience was off to a great start for these two facts alone, but I was soon to learn how difficult life can be when surviving on little to no income. My mother had encouraged me to focus on my academics that first semester, and advised strongly against taking a part-time job. In all fairness, this decision probably saved my college career in the long run, but that semester I lived on cup noodles and not much else.

I was not academically prepared for college, especially with regards to my research and writing skills. This was well before the advent of the internet, so I had to become book savvy fast. I quickly fell in love with the library, where I spent long spells between classes. It became a second home to me that first year. Even though I was never a strong reader, books had always fascinated me. As bizarre as it sounds, I love the feel and smell of old books—the older, the better. I could never explain it, but wandering the stacks and burying my nose in the pages of an old book brought me much-needed moments of tranquility, and walking back to my dormitory after a long study session gave me a refreshing sense of accomplishment. Mostly, I relished the quiet environment that the library provided. I could sit in a study carrel for hours at a time with my books, paper, and pen, hidden away from the world and filling my mind with knowledge. It was a feeling that I had never before experienced on such a level. I also relied heavily on the student writing center for assistance with the revision and editing process. I never had any difficulty getting my thoughts down on paper, but the conventions still haunt me to this day. If I hadn't buckled down and forced myself to focus and accept help, I would have failed out of school in my first year.

Given that I was accruing upwards of twenty-thousand dollars a year in student loans, I really wish my academic advisor had told me that it was unlikely that I would be financially successful as a history major. I had decided on history because I enjoyed learning about different cultures and societies. The other reason was that I thought it would be romantic to grow a long beard, wear cardigans, smoke a pipe, and talk about how events of the past had shaped the present. I spent days copying the words dictated by my professors. I might have been better served in a career as a court stenographer.

A week before each exam, my professors would hand out a study guide with potential essay topics. I spent countless hours in the library studying and writing practice essays. Some nights, I fell asleep at my study carrel, only to be awoken by the librarian at closing time. I would thank her as I wiped the drool from my mouth and notes. Examination day always found me in a robotic state, regurgitating information word for word from my memory until I filled the examination booklet. It was a horrific study method and I would never advise it, but it was all I knew. My professors were impressed, but it was exhausting.

The library was a welcome respite from my rooming situation. Although my roommates were all pals of mine, our dorm was no larger than the average single-occupant bedroom, and there were four of us crammed in there, all at the mind-boggling age of eighteen. Privacy was next to impossible to come by. I will leave the implications to your imagination. We slept on two bunk beds stacked side by side against the one wall. I bunked on the top with Big Red, who snored loud enough to keep the entire dormitory awake, underneath me. It was quite an adjustment that first semester, with many sleepless nights. Beef slept feet-to-feet with me on the top of the other bunk, with Scooter below him.

Big Red, Beef, and I were fairly open-minded fellas during our freshman year at college, but Scooter was a conservative good old boy. The look on his face when Big Red and Beef told him that they'd gotten an adult movie stuck in his VCR was priceless. Turnabout being fair play, the looks on Beef and Big Red's faces when Scooter's dad fixed the VCR and gave them their tape back were even better. He survived an entire year with three of the most dysfunctional minds at the college, but that said, it took him only a week to hang blankets up around his bunk like curtains to shield himself from our madness. I don't blame him. How could he sleep? We ate more damn pizza while watching more television under the glow of more black lights at earlier hours of the morning than anyone else I knew. He rarely yelled at us, except for the time we burned holes in the carpet that his parents had provided us with. He also occasionally became outwardly angry if we "accidentally" got into his snacks in the middle of the night. They were stowed away in the darkest corner of his wardrobe, so in all fairness it was tough to justify our thievery.

All in all, though, he was a grand sport about it. I would have been at the hall director's door asking for a room change after a week. He was a ball player, a local legend in rural parts of Pennsylvania. He once showed me the newspaper clipping about a no-hitter he'd pitched in high school. He was quite proud of his accomplishments, but humble in his expression of his feats. I admired that quality.

We tried to eat breakfast in the dormitory to save funds. Beef, a self-proclaimed barista, would wake us to the sound of grinding coffee beans. A cigarette with coffee was his usual choice of breakfast. The guy looked like Jesus, grinding beans in his boxer shorts. Even better, his coffee pot only made one cup.

Scooter was a cereal eater, and clanked his spoon on the bottom of the bowl with every bite. The guy would sit there, clanking his way through a bowl of Fruit Loops like there was no tomorrow, wearing an honest-to-god banana hammock. He had no reservations about showing everyone his rear-end before breakfast, so we started each day with a full moon. Big Red never took an early class, but he would often wake us up with his snoring or a canyon-shot explosion of gas. I just sat back like a fly on the wall and soaked it all in.

YOU WEAR WHAT?

Scooter's damn underwear served as the token of quite a few interesting moments during that first year of college, but perhaps the most notable of these occurred in my second semester when I had to take a public speaking course. I do not enjoy speaking in front of others. To this day the only way I can feel comfortable in speaking situations is to rely on my warped sense of humor. An audience will forgive a lot if you can get them to laugh. Our first assignment was to teach the class a new skill or activity. I didn't have many skills that could be taught in the space of five minutes, or at least, none that I thought would amuse my classmates. But luckily, I did know someone who could help. Barlow was a country music dancer—we had met through a mutual friend in first semester and I had gone line dancing with him a few times—so I asked him to teach me an easy dance known as "The Watermelon Crawl." After several practice sessions, I had the steps down and was feeling extremely confident. He allowed me the use of his cowboy boots, black Stetson hat, and boom box as props for my speech. My hope was that by making the class get out of their seats and comfort zones, my nerves would not be so apparent.

When the day came, I made the class stand up and complete each individual step with me in order to loosen things up. Then I put on the Stetson and fired up the boom box. People were really getting into it, laughing at their own awkwardness, and that of our professor, who had joined in. During the second run through, I began a rhythmic clap that caught on quickly. I ended by whirling my Stetson into the air and let loose a jovial cowboy cry. Success! The speech had provided me with a foundation to build upon, and I felt more at ease with the process.

The second assignment was a persuasive speech, in which we had to influence the audience to choose one object over another. My mind went straight to Scooter's grape smugglers. I knew I could offer several convincing points as to why it was more beneficial for men to wear boxer briefs instead of what amounted to a roomy thong. However, I did not want to steal Scooter's underwear, so I simply explained my thought process regarding the speech and he gladly obliged, offering me his finest tiger-striped banana hammock. In addition to the ludicrous drawers, I took with me a pair of my own boxer briefs. I planned on using myself as a visual aide for points of emphasis.

I focused my presentation on the comfort of the two types of underwear. I wore a pair of jogging pants to class that day over a borrowed a pair of baseball sliding shorts. Sliding shorts go under a baseball player's pants to offer an extra layer of padding when sliding on the diamond. I was going to use the tight-fitting shorts as my primary layer. I would drop my jogging pants a minute into the speech and model the two distinct cuts over top of the sliding shorts. As my professor and about half of the students in the class were female, I wanted to make sure that my speech didn't come across as offensive, so I practiced the night before in front of one of my favorite people in the world, Bella, and her three roommates. Bella and I had met when her older sister dated my older brother during their freshman year of high school, and after learning that we shared a love of sports we'd struck up a friendship that lasted long after our respective siblings broke up. Bella was an amazing softball player, even making the college team as a catcher. We always joked that if we were both single at thirty, we would get hitched.

I slid the tiger-striped grape smugglers over my sliding shorts and covered them with my jogging pants, before introducing my topic to the four young women in their dorm. They sat on the two lower bunks eating popcorn while I took up my presentation in the center of the room. I had a little difficulty getting through my introduction, because the ladies were already frenzied with excitement over my topic. For a brief moment, I felt like a Chip N' Dale dancer with all the shrieking. I did my best to maintain my composure and went into my points of persuasion. "Comfort," I began. "How is a garment like this supposed to be comfortable?" With that, I dropped my jogging pants and stood there baring my sliding shorts and the tiger-striped banana hammock. Composure, I told myself, as the girls screeched with glee. I started in with my points about the cut of the underwear—simply too high in the front and the back. I could already feel a line forming across my lower buttocks, like the one I used to get across my waistband as a kid whenever I started to outgrow my drawers.

"Furthermore," I continued, "the cut is such that the waistband will inevitably ride even higher when the wearer takes a seat. It's hard enough to sit still and focus," I argued, "without being wedgied by your own underpants." I paused for a moment, letting the visual run its course. Then, I turned my attention to the front of the underwear and offered an uncomfortable glance, followed by a simple statement: "The cut is too damn high." I went into a monologue about the restriction of movement and overall lack of breathability. "In addition to the lack of comfort," I posited, "outside of the world of male dancers, who in their right mind wears underwear like this?" All these points I addressed with the straightest face and calmest tone of voice I could manage. Bella and her roommates nodded their heads in support, while hiding their giggles behind cupped hands.

Afterward, I traded out my tiger-striped grape smugglers for the more comfortable boxer briefs. I stressed the wider band, which would eliminate any pressure marks along the waist, even turning to demonstrate how the boxer brief did not cut across my lower buttocks. "No red lines or marks here," I stated.

Additionally, I pointed out that not all men are blessed with beautiful, muscular upper thighs, and so the boxer briefs were ideal for covering the skinny frog legs of us less fortunate fellows. My confidence grew as I chewed over the breathability and comfort points. Bella and her roommates gave me a standing ovation as I concluded my presentation with a three-sixty turn in my boxer briefs and flung the tiger-striped grape smugglers over my left shoulder.

The next day, I anxiously awaited my turn to speak in class. My leg kept jiggling under my desk, and the grape smugglers were riding up my left butt cheek to the point that I wanted to pick it out. My stomach churned and I was sweating profusely. The last thought that ran through my mind as I at last approached the front of the class was that this speech was either going to be a masterpiece or an utter embarrassment. I was at the point of no return. The introduction went off smoothly. So far, so good, I told myself. I had my professor giggling, and my classmates shaking their heads in disbelief. Then I dropped my jogging pants. It took the audience a minute to regain their composure as I stood stone-faced, giving the necessary wait time before continuing with my presentation. A tiger print banana hammock over athletic spanx was the stuff that second tier superheroes are made of.

I had found my voice in public speaking, and it has withstood the test of time. I haven't resorted to dropping my trousers since that occasion, but humor remains a vital tool in my speech-writing arsenal even now. My professor offered high praise for my gamble, and I wore those tiger-print undies under my jogging pants proudly as I walked back to my dormitory with my head held high.

A CHANGE OF SCENERY

Spring break of my sophomore year I took a road trip that sent me down an unforeseen path. I had now ground my way through three semesters of college and had spent the better half of my sophomore year living in the basement of a house near campus. My accommodations and needs were minimal during that year. I was still driving my old rusty red truck, and I had gotten a job working for minimum wage as a stock boy at one of the last remaining Woolworth Department stores. My first day on the job, the manager packed me a ham and cheese sandwich because I looked "like a skeleton." I'd gotten the sense that she was eyeing me up and down during my interview, lit cigarette dangling from her mouth, but I wouldn't have guessed that that was what she was thinking.

On top of my full load of classes, I was working twenty hours a week, which gave me enough money to cover rent, gas for Rusty Red, and a week's worth of ramen noodles. There were six fellas who resided and paid rent in the house. The chief tenant had taken a liking to me and took me under his wing. He watched out for me like an older brother during my time there. I paid fifty dollars a month to live in the basement. Two old crusty couches pulled together served as my bed, and I spent many a winter night praying to the Lord that this musty basement would not be my coffin as I listened to the old furnace flicker and spark like bugs getting too close to a zap light. The fellas had twin black cats that came and went on the heels of the many friends who frequented the house from campus, and wreaked havoc on the other cats in the neighborhood. Some mornings I woke to them cozied under my covers. The house was lively at all hours of the night, so it was a blessing to be sleeping in the basement. Despite the loud yelling, laughter, and noise of people on the floor above, I could usually muster a few hours of sleep.

It was far from perfect, but at this point in my life it was home. Big Red had dropped out of school after a year to load trucks at the local UPS hub. He initially planned to just take a semester off, but he never returned to college. I saw less and less of Scooter after I left the dorms, but we passed occasionally on the way to class. Beef, however, also lived in the house, and had helped secure me the spot in the basement.

I was nineteen, restless, and in desperate need of a change of scenery when spring break crept up on me. Outside of family vacations, I had not been outside of the Midwest, but Beef had convinced me to go with him on a trip to Florida. I was short on dough but as always, Beef looked out for me. Our dear friend Bruiser, who was a defensive end for the college football team, tagged along for the ride. We borrowed the reverend's Jesus Chrysler for the trip.

Bruiser, Beef, and I take in one final glorious sunrise before making the long drive back to Cleveland.

The good reverend was Beef's pop and one of the greatest souls I ever had the privilege of meeting. Yes, he was an actual reverend. I was introduced to Revy, as he was affectionately known, during Big Red and Beef's high school graduation. Throughout our first two years of college, Revy and JuJu (Beef's mom) would often meet us halfway between central Ohio and the college to take us out to an amazing dinner. They were the type of people that one was better for knowing. The dear reverend always afforded us the opportunity to make our mistakes, but would offer insight into our mishaps as a means of teaching us how to be better men. I always felt closer to God after a good heart-to-heart with the reverend.

That automobile didn't drive down the interstate, it floated. So in the middle of March, a magnificent trio of Beef, Bruiser, and myself headed down the interstate to Florida. Ten hours into the trip on the first day, we pulled off into a backwoods campground in North Carolina well past sunset and just managed to pitch a tent in the dark and build a fire before passing out. We awoke to a glorious Carolina sunrise. We weren't due to arrive in Florida for another two days, so we opted for a quick detour to Duke Power State Park. The plan was to hang out for a day and enjoy the weather. Little did I know, the next twenty-four hours would impact the next decade of my life.

Duke Power was an hour's drive away. I was mesmerized by the landscape. The rolling hills of the Piedmont were vastly open compared to the cookie cutter plots of Cleveland, and gigantic pines lined the road like stoic sentries of the land. The sunny seventy-degree weather had us all in great spirits. We pulled the Jesus Chrysler into the state park and I watched as Beef backed over the wooden post that marked camp site number twenty-nine. We laughed hysterically, inane with a feverish excitement that had been locked away in the morbid winter weather. As we were flinging a Frisbee back and forth, a ranger pulled up to collect our campsite dues. We chatted it up for a minute before she wished us a safe and enjoyable trip.

The rest of that day found Beef, Bruiser, and I frolicking along the park trails. We waded into the lake up to our waists and laid out along the banks for hours, looking up at the cloudless blue sky. It was during that period of euphoria that I made the decision that I was finished with the harsh weather and depressed routine that I had fallen into during the last few years in Cleveland. Relaxing in this surreal landscape had given me the clarity I was searching for. Beef snapped a photo of me standing knee deep in the lake, gazing out over the placid, glittering water with my hands laced behind my head and an expression of utter peace on my face. When we looked at that photograph a few days after we returned, Beef told me that our time at Duke Power was the happiest he had ever seen me. It only served to reaffirm my decision.

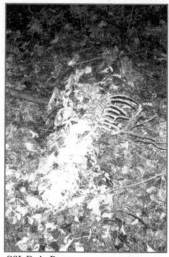

CSI: Duke Power

As afternoon faded into dusk, we started making our way back to camp through the trees, only to nearly trip over the decaying carcass of a deer. City boys that we were, we were immediately convinced that this deer must have been mauled by a bear. We crouched over the remains like a trio of CSI investigators, looking for claw and bite marks. It's a good thing no one was around to hear our analysis, because we had absolutely no idea what we were talking about. Still, our close examination fed our anxiety, which sent us back to our campsite at a full-tilt sprint.

That night we sat around the campfire toasting s'mores and talking nonsense. The stars lit the sky like a path toward heaven. As I sat there, soaking in the modest scale of my existence, Bruiser brought me crashing back to reality with a panicked scream of "Bears, bears!" Beef and I needed no further prompting to follow him in a mad dash for safety behind the doors of the Jesus Chrysler, only to watch three gigantic raccoons come waddling out of the trees to rummage around our campsite. City boys. Our tent was filled with laughter over our own folly that night. We awoke the next morning to the ransacked remains of our cooler and snack stash, courtesy of one of the three resident bears of Duke Power State Park. Every new experience during the remainder of the trip down to Florida and back further illuminated the small fishbowl of my life.

I knew in my heart that it was time for a change.

After our return to Cleveland, I went to the bookstore and looked up universities in North Carolina, eventually settling on the University of North Carolina at Greensboro. I based my decision solely on which school had the greatest female-to-male ratio— not the most scholarly way to choose a university, but I was nineteen and desperate to get out of Cleveland. In retrospect, I don't think it would have mattered what school I attended in North Carolina. I just needed a new path. The problem was that I had been accepted and enrolled in a university that I had yet to visit and knew nothing about. I was betting on myself and the winds of fate.

WHERE YOU GOING?

The rest of the semester before I transferred was fairly uneventful. The only hiccup occurred when I rifled a baseball through my friend's rear windshield during a game of catch. The silver lining was that I had started speaking with my pops again. I needed four hundred dollars to replace the broken window, and Dad, true to who he is, didn't hesitate for a minute.

As summer inched closer, I made the decision to go live with my father to help him put a new roof on his cottage near Lake Erie. I knew I was leaving at summer's end and although we'd made up, we were both still in need of closure. I missed him. I was ready to turn the page on the next chapter of my life, and I wanted him to be a part of it. In the end, I didn't do a whole lot of physical work on the roof, but we were able to repair our damaged relationship. Between minimally helping Dad and some side gigs doing landscaping, I also managed to make enough money that I didn't need to take a steady job the next year.

That summer was a bittersweet time for me. It took three years, but my family was back together, if not quite the same as it had been before. The anger from the divorce had softened as we moved forward, each in our own way. I spent a lot of time that summer lost in reflection about my life in Cleveland. It was difficult to rationalize my sudden wanderlust, except to say that some driving force deep in my consciousness was pushing me toward a new beginning. Most evenings I would walk the half block to the lake and watch the sunset over the lapping shore break. I had a thousand conversations with myself about my purpose in life and giving myself a chance to fulfill my dreams. To be young, alive, and moving toward change lifted my spirits. I had been stuck in a rut for far too long.

In early August, Mom and her fiancé at the time took me to visit the University of North Carolina. I was to register for classes and attend the new student orientation. About twenty miles outside of Greensboro, my mother asked me where the university was located, and I was forced to admit that I had no idea where the university was and that I basically knew nothing about the school except the female-to-male student ratio was two to one. Mom just shook her head while her fiancé chuckled. She understood, more than most, that I needed to get away. In fact, it made touring the university a genuine experience for all of us. My first impressions of UNCG were promising. The campus was beautiful, and so were the people. I instantly fell in love with southern accents.

A few weeks later, my father and Frank drove me from Cleveland to Greensboro in a loaded-down Chevy Cavalier. Like our father, Frank and I had put our past behind us. We were family. They helped me unpack, took me to dinner, and wished me well. Lying on my bed the first night with the window to my dorm room open, not knowing a single person in the entire state, let alone on campus, I was truly alone. My decision to start over had officially gone into effect. Thoughts flooded my mind as I attempted to find comfort in the solitude of my dreams, but I couldn't help but wonder if I had made a huge mistake.

My first few weeks at UNCG were some of the loneliest days of my life. It took me five minutes to realize that my new roommate and I were a poor match. I was trying to find my way and he was looking for the next party. I spent an extraordinary amount of time at the university's exercise facility. I lifted more weights and ran more miles around the track that first week than I had in the last decade. I contacted the school housing department and secured a transfer into the international academic dorm. It was the only dormitory that had availability. It was awkward but interesting to watch the interactions of students from different countries in their quest to learn English.

I was paired up with a quiet Korean kid who was only at UNCG for a semester to develop his English language skills. He was quiet, respectful, and a hell of a mathematician, which worked out perfectly because I was taking the only math class required for my degree that semester. I was a horrific math student in high school and college. I had figured out a way to memorize facts about history, but math was a different story. I was solid with basic computation and algebra, but I got lost somewhere around Algebra II and Geometry. However, with the tutelage of my roommate, I was shooting for the stars. I floundered my way valiantly to the final exam and was ecstatic to earn a C. I spent a lot time with my new roommate and his two Korean friends, who lived next door. They were hysterical, even though most of the time I had no comprehension of what they were saying. Yet, they cordially invited me to join them in all of their plans. We played cards and they smoked cigarettes most nights. I have never seen anyone chain smoke the way those boys did. In return for their kindness, I tried my best to help out with their English studies. They were funny as hell in the way they tried to put their word combinations together. I taught them a few catchy phrases: "Get your ducks in a row," and "It takes sunshine and rain to make a rainbow." But the cursing was by far the best. They got all the words in the wrong order, but it was just too funny to correct.

One weekend in early October, I decided to meet up with an old friend of mine, Monroe, who was living in Raleigh for a year painting houses with his pops. Our plan was to drive to the Appalachian Trail and spend a few days in the mountains. My Korean friends took the same long weekend to head out to the coast and see the Atlantic Ocean. I was slightly concerned by the amount of booze they were taking along, but I figured they were just going to blow off some steam at a run-down hotel near the beach.

Monroe and I spent three gorgeous nights sleeping in a cabin on the trail near the Tennessee-Carolina border. The mice ran across the rafters above our heads every night, and I hadn't thought to bring a sleeping bag with me, only the comforter off my bed, which I ruined. But aside from freezing my backside off, the hiking, views, and autumn foliage were fabulous. I hadn't seen Monroe in about a year, so it was great to catch up.

When I got back to campus Sunday afternoon, my Korean friends were nowhere to be found. I thought nothing of it. I made my way to the library and chow hall for some studying and dinner. When I returned to the dormitory at twilight, there was still no sign of my new-found friends. I went to bed concerned but rationalized that something must have come up. They would eventually resurface, I told myself.

I went to class on Monday and returned to the dorm shortly after lunch to find my three Korean friends huddled in the room next door, all with expressions ranging from stress to sheer panic on their faces. I immediately knew that something must have gone drastically wrong on their trip, but I only began to really piece things together when they handed me the card for a lawyer and asked me to please call him. I did so and soon found myself serving as a makeshift interpreter, and slowly the story came out. Apparently, the boys had decided to start drinking while driving down the highway, and about an hour from their beach destination, they were pulled over. The car had been swerving between both lanes at a blistering thirty miles per hour. They were in a bit of trouble.

The boys were mesmerized by the flashing lights and had decided to take pictures of the police cruiser pulling them over. Their high level of intoxication and amateur photography did not sit too well with the officer. After the initial stop, the boys were made to lie face down on the side of the highway. This too, they found hysterical, along with the process of being frisked, failing a roadside sobriety test, getting handcuffed, and being taken to the station. Upon their arrival at the police station, they were cuffed to a railing on a bench to await their booking. They continued to photograph the process as if visiting a tourist attraction. On the bright side, it was apparently around this point that the officers began to realize just how little English my Korean friends actually understood and started to see the humor in the situation.

They spent the night in the drunk tank and awoke the following morning with severe headaches, baffled by their surroundings. The driver of the car, and by far the eldest of the three, was facing the most serious consequences. His BAC was significantly over the legal limit and he was concerned about losing his study visa. My other two friends received a ticket for disorderly conduct. Fortunately, all three of their families were well off and they had secured an excellent lawyer, with whom I became very well acquainted over the course of the next week. The driver was allowed to finish his semester abroad, as it was his intention to return to Korea at the end of the semester anyway. He was in his late thirties and was mainly studying at the university for the experience of living in the United States. He paid a hefty fine, and I'm sure his driver's license was revoked. My current roommate was returning to Korea at the end of the semester as well. He also paid a fine for his role in the ordeal. My third friend and future roommate also paid a fine but was allowed to continue his studies at the university. The whole incident was pretty funny in retrospect. The boys took me out to a Korean restaurant as a thank-you for helping them out.

THE ONE CALLED YUN

The first time I actually met Yun, he was sleeping on the floor of the communal shower, snoring loudly and smelling strongly of alcohol. I had woken up and was heading for my morning trip to the restroom when I spotted him. I just chuckled before using the facilities. I brushed my teeth, washed up for class, and walked past him again on my way out. I truly have no idea how long he slept there, but I have to admit, the kid intrigued me.

Yun moved in with me at the end of the semester, bringing along his collection of rap CD's, a quacking duck alarm clock, and his pack-a-day Marlboro Light habit. He was the only one of my three Korean friends to remain at the end of the first semester. Yun was always walking around with headphones on, singing along to English rap lyrics with a cigarette dangling from his lips. The guy was seriously into the latest fashions. He loved to shop and take trips to American tourist destinations during holiday breaks.

Yun's comic relief was a breath of fresh air from the daily grind of university life. I didn't realize it until years later, but we needed each other in that particular moment. I was always mixed up in some girlfriend drama or other during those years at UNCG, and Yun kept me grounded in perspective. I can be overly emotional, clinging to the highs and lows of each day, but my boy was always there for me through thick and thin. Most nights that I stayed at the dorm, Yun and I ended the day with a bowl of hot noodles and a smoke. I learned a great deal about his upbringing and the culture of South Korea, and through a bizarre set of circumstances made a true friend. My sole regret was that I didn't hang out with him more. He missed his family immensely and I should have put his friendship first. Still, I did my best to offer assistance with his English studies. He was a fast learner. Yun's fluency grew by leaps and bounds during that year we lived together. The following fall, he was accepted into the university as a full-time student.

My dear friend Yun and me, shortly after graduation.

I was a twenty-year-old college kid and wasn't always thinking straight, but even after I moved out the next year to live with my girlfriend at the time, we stayed in touch and still hung out. Yun attended my graduation and even helped me move to Wilmington that summer. He graduated from UNCG with both an undergraduate and master's degree in economics. We drifted apart with time, as so many do, so I can only speculate that he must have returned to South Korea at some point. His friendship was one of the greatest gifts that I ever received in my life. I regret that I never got the opportunity to really tell him how much he meant to me.

CHLOE

In my last few years of college, a beautiful blonde Carolina girl captivated my heart, and I moved in with her my senior year at UNCG. Our apartment was in a massive manor house that had been divided into four units. Hands down, it was the best place I have ever lived. Everything about the century-old home resonated as vintage south. We lived in the upstairs two-bedroom apartment, which had hardwood floors, a great side balcony, and a screened-in porch off the back of the house. For a while, life was smooth sailing—going to classes and working at the YMCA, the parking lot of which bordered the back of the property. A lazy southern summer arrived, and life slowed into a routine of work and wine-filled dinners. Weekends were spent on short excursions that kept life interesting, until the day we decided to go to the North Carolina state fair.

We had gone the year before, but only lasted an hour because I made the rookie mistake of downing a smoked sausage hoagie before attempting to ride the Salt and Pepper Shaker. I was hell bent on not ruining this year's trip. It was beautiful until we visited the local farmer section of the fair and chatted it up with a likeable Carolina farmer, a rather portly individual wearing overalls, a sweat-stained t-shirt, and a straw hat, who was holding an adorable miniature pig. His wide, unshaven face was shadowed with stubble and his smile was as wide as his belly. The moment my girl saw those little oinkers, I knew we were in a world of trouble. Sure enough, we paid the likeable gentlemen fifty bucks and departed the state fair with a five-pound black and white baby pot belly pig that we named Chloe. I knew it was a terrible idea. My god, a pig in an apartment. This is what young love does to people.

I would love to say the adventures with Chloe lasted a long time, but it was only a few months before life really began to unravel. To her credit, Chloe was an extremely intelligent pig. She mastered the litter box in under a week and I came to think of her as a sort of hybrid between a pig and a cat. But eventually, the noise of her little hooves on the hardwood floor made our downstairs neighbors—and our landlord—a bit curious. The message was quite clear: either the pig leaves, or we do. So, we did what any young couple in love would do in that situation: we walked out on our lease and found a house for rent that was willing to accept our pet.

Chloe rousing me with her snout from an afternoon nap.

We ended up renting a three-bedroom house in a rougher part of Greensboro. We were a few miles from the YMCA, and I rode my skateboard to school since we only had one car. I had been messing around with skateboards since I was a kid, but I never was into the tricks or the ramps. I just loved the glide and the sound of the wheels on the pavement. Still, it wasn't long before we were forced to admit that we had bit off more than we could financially chew. Chloe continued to grow at a rapid pace, and soon outgrew her litterbox. I have since learned that this is a common misconception when people are sold pet pigs—they're billed as "mini" or "pygmy," and people assume this means they'll grow to be roughly the size of a small dog. In truth, the terms are relative to the size of farm pigs, which are truly massive, so a full-grown potbelly pig, while certainly not small, is technically "miniature" by comparison. Not that it helps to know that when you have one living in your house.

We were so strapped for cash that winter that we didn't have enough money to turn the heat on. Instead, we borrowed a couple of kerosene heaters in an attempt to keep the house warm enough to inhabit. It did not work. The stress of keeping Chloe, on top of our financial situation, led to the temporary downfall of our relationship. We left Chloe at my friend Reggie's farm for the holidays and each returned home to our families. I spent the flight mulling over whether to end my relationship and drop out of UNCG, and by the end of winter break I was determined to do both.

I drove my mom's car back to Greensboro with the intention of dropping out of school and returning home to Cleveland, and I did in fact drop out for a day. While staying at Reggie's farm for a few days, however, I came to the realization that I had come too far to give up on my goals. I was going to finish my degree at UNCG and continue what I started when I left Cleveland. I drove back to campus and reenrolled for the second semester of my senior year. I drove my mom's car all the way back to Cleveland and hopped a Greyhound bus back to Carolina. In the end, we lost the house and Chloe. She was sent to live with my girlfriend's relatives in southern Virginia. They were chicken farmers with fifty acres, and Chloe was allowed to live out the duration of her life. She became best friends with the family dog and the two made a dynamic duo for quite a few years. She made it to the ripe old age of nine and weighed over two hundred pounds at the time of her death.

The reality of my decision really hit home during that four-teen-hour bus ride back to North Carolina. I had quit my job at the YMCA when I thought I was returning to Cleveland. I was twenty years old, essentially homeless, and still a solid year away from graduation.

THE FARM

I first met Reggie while working as a camp counselor at the YMCA, and since my life was going sideways at the time, he soon became a surrogate father to me. After returning to Greensboro, having quit my job and lost my house, I was at least able to reconcile with my girlfriend. However, in light of recent events her parents had forbidden us from living together, so I could only crash at her studio apartment intermittently. The rest of the time, I stayed with Reggie, Mama T, and the rest of their family on the farm.

It was during my time at the farm that I unearthed a latent love for the rural lifestyle hidden deep inside my soul. The property was forty acres, and I spent a great deal of time there in isolation, roaming the pastures and trails. It was vastly open, different from any place I had ever lived. I would disappear for hours to hunt squirrels with an air rifle, only to walk into that old farmhouse at sunset emptyhanded. I just enjoyed the solitude and tranquility the land offered. It was during this period in my life that I began to realize the power of my emotions and how drastically they swayed my thoughts and actions on a daily basis.

I had lost my job at the YMCA due to unreliability, what with all my coming and going between Greensboro and Cleveland, so I worked odd jobs on the farm helping Mama T and Reggie where needed. I also helped Mama T out with the tile business that she and Reggie ran on the side to make ends meet. We mainly did residential work, tiling bathroom floors and countertops. I spent my days running up and down stairs to the tile saw. It wasn't the most enjoyable work, but it put a little cigarette money in my pocket. For the time being, that was all I truly needed. I spent my last two years at UNCG writing most of my history papers in the living room of the farmhouse. When I finished typing up my final paper for my degree, having spent the night chain-smoking between strong cups of coffee, the only one up to celebrate with me was the ghost of Reggie's grandpa, who made sure to let me know he was present.

I never believed in ghosts until I lived at the farm. Mama T had a unique ability to see and communicate with these entities, and none of the spirits on the farm were malicious. In fact, according to Reggie and Mama T, they were mostly departed relatives who had lived and died on the property. Reggie's grandpa had died in the corner of the kitchen where the table with the coffee pot now sat. Apparently, his bed was there during the final chapter of his life. He was the spirit that I encountered most often, usually late at night.

Reggie's grandmother was another frequent visitor. She had a particular fondness for the younger of Reggie's two daughters. I would often hear stories sitting around the kitchen table of encounters between the two. I was graced with grandma's presence once when I was home alone drinking coffee and listening to Stevie Ray Vaughn on full volume in the living room. Ten minutes into my jam fest, a wooden doll, which had been situated over on the mantel piece, landed a few feet from me. It must have traveled at least twenty feet through the air, and I was nowhere near that mantle. In fact, I was halfway through a spin move and an air guitar solo when it clattered to the hardwood floor. Rooted to the spot, I felt the hair on the back of my neck stand on end as I issued a meek apology to the eerie tension that suddenly filled the room. I knew I was not alone. I took a deep breath and made a dash out the side door, where I stayed for over an hour waiting for Mama T to arrive.

When at last she pulled into the driveway, I greeted her

before she could even open the driver side door and emphatically explained my dilemma. She chuckled and told me that I must have pissed off Grandma playing my music too loud. It had happened to her a couple of times over the course of the last year.

Mama T and Reggie told me about some of the other spirits who had made their presence known on the homestead, so I dug in to do some research, being the so-called historian in the house. The farm had been in the family since before the Civil War. The original farmhouse included the kitchen, living room, and the front two bedrooms. An addition was built in the early 1920's, but I never had any personal experiences with the entities in the new part of the house.

The farm had everything I could ever have envisioned, dreaming of a life in the rural south. The road to the farm was a steep, meandering dirt lane that cut through the woods before opening onto the ten acres upon which the homestead was built. The two-story farmhouse was paneled with white plank boards atop an old stone foundation. There were front and side porch entries, but the screened-in porch off the master bedroom was breathtaking. It overlooked the barn and the main pasture. I loved autumn on the farm. The wind whipping through the glorious changing leaves and across the pastures sent a sense of peace resonating within me. I spent many chilly fall evenings sitting on that porch, learning to play guitar.

Reggie's farm was picture-perfect. The barn was faded red with white trim and a massive sliding front door and even a hayloft on the second level. I was captivated by the weathered boards, the potent smell of the cattle, and the barn swallows that dove in and out of the open door. As a kid, I had always been fascinated by calendars of farm life; old barns and privies and stately farmhouses. My time on Reggie's farm awakened something in me that had been dormant for a decade. The rustic solitude of my new surroundings was well worth the modern conveniences I had left behind. I sometimes dreamt of converting the loft into a modest apartment for myself and staying there forever.

Walking across the dirt lane from the barn toward the farmhouse offered a view of the old well and smokehouse. The smokehouse served as a storage shed and trophy case of relics from days long gone. Timeworn tools hung from rusty nails pounded into the log walls, serving as inspiration to those who currently occupied the land; a tribute to the diligent efforts put forth by previous generations. In true farm fashion, the well drew such poor water pressure that the toilets were only ever flushed for obvious reasons. The lone shower was upstairs and supplied enough running water for approximately two minutes at a time. The shower head was equipped with a switch to cut the water on and off. Most people would cringe at amenities such as these, but I was intrigued by the rustic means. A successful shower depended on how quickly I could get wet before cutting off the switch. I'd scrub up quickly, especially in winter months, with the water off, then cut it back on when I was done. Then, it was a race to rinse all the soap off of my body before the water ran out again. Hot water was intermittent at best, so winter showers were often brutal. As such, true showers only happened once or twice a week. The rest of the time, I made do with birdy baths.

The farmhouse was surrounded by open fields for several acres before reaching the tree line. At one time, these had been wheat and corn fields, but Reggie let them grow wild and kept a family garden for vegetables off the side of the house. I often found myself tending the vegetable patch late in the afternoons, tugging at stubborn weeds. The land spoke to me for reasons I could not explain. The high grasses still held that majestic quality, blowing in the breeze of a late summer evening. Across the front yard and adjacent to the farm was a row of gigantic pines that stood like ancient sentries, overlooking the pasture next to the barn. The pasture was a grand, wide open space of approximately fifteen acres, broken up only by narrow ridgelines of woods that separated the fields. Several acres across from the stoic pines stood the enormous hay bales used to feed the cattle during the winter months. Among these stood an old dead oak with limbs like outstretched arms, which always made me think of Halloween.

Many nights I would stroll out of that old farmhouse and cross over the lane to sit in solitude on a bench under the last pine closest to the barn, and just stare out across the pasture at the dead oak and the hay bales. It was here that I did some of my most profound thinking and even held a number of arguments with myself. I didn't have much to really be contemplating, sitting there with only twenty-one years' worth of triumphs and tragedies behind me, but I had a lot to figure out.

One night, Mama T's son Wayne swung by the farm to hang out for an evening. He was a talented guitar player but struggled to find direction in his life. Under the shadows of that old oak, silhouetted spookily against the full moon, Wayne and I climbed the haystacks together with a pack of Lucky Strikes and a bottle of whiskey in tow. It's a miracle that we didn't catch fire to the entire stack of hay bales. For the next few hours, we were kings of the night and the world ceased to exist. We shared stories of frustration, alternating roles between speaker and listener. We asked questions like, "What causes people to hate?" and "Is there a God?" We expressed our hopes and dreams for our lives. Fueled by the whiskey, we delved deeper and deeper into the fears that held us back, as intense and meaningful dialogue gave way to drunken ramblings.

At one point we both stood and howled at the silhouette of the full moon. Snake-bit with whiskey, I decided that night that I was not going to let another person ever dictate my journey in life. I was bound and determined to make my own way in this world. I had spent too many sleepless nights letting others interfere with my happiness. In a drunken stupor, I declared, "I am the creator of my own happiness," to which Wayne nodded his head like he was listening to a spitfire preacher delivering a passionate sermon. "I am the only one that can hold me back." More nods from Wayne. "I will find my way in this world!"

I stood with that final declaration and promptly fell backward off the haystack and directly into a patch of brush. My tumble signified that we had consumed enough liquor for one night, so together, arm in arm, Wayne and I stumbled back across the pasture. Those few acres felt like miles as we muttered drunken support to each other like two wounded soldiers trying to make their way back from the front. The whiskey had us speaking in hushed voices. I guess we were worried we might wake the cows. I wasn't worried about being drunk in front of Reggie and Mama T, but I was paranoid about walking into the single wire electrical fence that kept the cows in pasture. Our mutual encouragement bolstered our confidence as we trekked on with arms outstretched.

I was just wondering aloud if the surge from the electric fence would be enough to kill us when, as if on cue, I felt the jolt of pain sear through my pant leg as I fell backward into the pasture. I was dead. Of that, I was certain, until I heard the distant cackles of Mama T and Reggie. They had gotten wise to our tomfoolery and had been watching us from the bench beneath the giant pines.

Twenty minutes later, I vomited profusely outside of the farmhouse, a gut-wrenching sickness that caused me to curse the drinking gods. I stumbled back into the living room, puke breath stinging in my eyes, and reaffirmed my declaration of freedom from an hour earlier. I knew I had just experienced a potentially life defining moment. Even if I was going to have a hell of a hangover come morning.

WILMINGTON

Two days after an anticlimactic graduation, I left Greensboro with an undergraduate degree in history and a minor in sociology. Needless to say, I spent the next few weeks beating back recruiters and headhunters with a stick. I knew I was in hot demand, as any other history, English, or art major can surely attest. My mom and I made the trek home from Greensboro to Cleveland in about ten hours. I drove the entire way and never was there a better conversation. She expressed her excitement and her admiration toward me for finishing my degree. We talked about my options and what I hoped to accomplish next in my life. I had left Cleveland because it was necessary for my growth, but I always enjoyed going home for the summer. We rolled into my mom's place in the early evening, and after unpacking, I decided to catch up on lost time with Big Red.

Pops helped me secure a lease on a new truck, and my old Italian friend, Tony, found me a gig for the summer. I was home for about a week when I received a call from an elementary school principal in Wilmington, North Carolina about a position as a teacher's assistant. Well, what could I do? I jumped in my new truck and drove twelve hours to the coast. I accepted the job, which was to begin with the start of the new school year. I was slated to make $15,000 a year. I wouldn't say it was ideal, but I had to move forward with my life. My girlfriend was shipping off to the Philippines to fulfill her lifelong dream of joining the Peace Corp, and I didn't want to spend a prolonged period of time back in the Cleveland. I had always thought of working in education, so I decided to work toward earning my teaching certification in the evenings while working as an assistant during the school day. At the end of the summer, I loaded up all of my worldly possessions in my new truck and voyaged back to North Carolina for the next chapter in my life.

I recruited my old friend Yun to help me move into my apartment, making a pit stop in Greensboro so he could follow me down to the coast. I pulled up to Yun's apartment and there he stood, leaning on his 1990 Honda Accord. I hadn't seen him in a few months, but he was the same old Yun: baseball cap on backwards, chain smoking Marlboros, with Korean rap pounding from his car speakers. We made the three-hour trek down the interstate toward Wilmington and pulled into my apartment complex late in the evening. It took us all of thirty minutes to unload my truck.

My dad had given me a love seat, a coffee table, an end table, a lamp, and a few pictures to take with me. The remainder of the truck was filled with clothes and personal essentials. I had a box of kitchen supplies that consisted of a few plates, cups, and silverware. I didn't have a bed yet, or furniture for my bedroom, but the love seat was supposed to pull out into a bed. Unfortunately, the pullout lay flat on the floor and was only a few inches thick, and my lower legs and feet hung off the end. I tried to sleep on it the first night after Yun left and decided I was better off sleeping on the little love seat itself. So all in all, my one-bedroom apartment was fairly empty. I ate, slept, and relaxed either on the love seat or on the floor. Not ideal, but I was making my way.

As I was bringing up the last of my clothes, Yun became determined to find the nearest Chinese buffet. Class act that he was, he had promised me dinner to celebrate my new job and place. We found it and proceeded to eat way too much food. For the remainder of the evening, we sat side by side on my love seat, drinking beers and reminiscing about our time together in Greensboro. I gave Yun the honor of sleeping on the love seat that first night while I used a blanket and a pillow and tried out the carpet on my living room floor. Of course, I slept not a wink between the nerves, Yun's snoring, and my stomach churning from too much Chinese food and beer.

I managed to pass out in the middle of the night, only to be awoken by a piercing scream a couple of hours later. I jolted awake to see the refrigerator door wide open, casting light on a bizarre scene: Yun, clad only in white briefs, crouched on the kitchen counter and cussing profusely in a mishmash of English and Korean. After a minute, I finally managed to piece together that he had seen a massive cockroach. He was dead set on finding a hotel to stay in for the night, and it took a great deal of coaxing and several Marlboro Lights before I could calm the big fella down enough to return to the love seat. He was still mumbling to himself as he fell back asleep. I considered pointing out that I was the one sleeping on the floor, but thought better of it.

The next day was to be Yun's last day in Wilmington, so we decided to go relax on the beach. On the way we stopped at a gas station and bought a huge inflatable raft. He spent the first hour on the beach alternating between blowing up the raft and smoking Marlboros in the knee-length athletic shorts he'd donned in lieu of swimwear. I sat on the beach, chuckling to myself as I watched my friend float atop his raft in the surf, smoking cigarettes and staring at the horizon like he was searching for something. I had never witnessed anyone smoking in the ocean before. At last, his portly frame came rumbling out of the surf, dragging his raft with a handful of cigarette butts. The next day, Yun returned to his life of Korean rap, Marlboro Lights, and coursework.

I sometimes wonder what Yun is up to these days. We didn't see much of each other after that. Wherever he is, I hope he's doing well for himself.

FRED SMITH

Everyone needs a Fred Smith to cross their path every so often to remind them what life should really be about. Fred walked into my life a few days after Yun returned to Greensboro. I heard it said once that a man should only count his true friends on one hand, and I will forever count Fred as one of mine. I was fortunate enough to be his teacher's assistant for two weeks, until the county sent him away to another school a few blocks away due to issues with the teacher/student ratio. But in those two weeks, I forged a friendship that has now lasted the better part of two decades. He is the greatest teacher, counselor, and thinker I have ever known; a man who is not afraid to live by his own set of rules and values.

Fred and I enjoying each other's company, as we did so often during our time together in Wilmington.

In his free time, Fred ran like the wind. I had been running for about three years when I met him—or so I thought.

Fred invited me to run with him one day after work. Although several years older than me, the guy frankly left me in the dust. He ran a five-mile loop around a cypress-lined lake faster than I could finish half of it. He walked home, took a shower, and came back just in time to meet me at the end of the trail. It was the only time I ever ran with Fred. He introduced me to the ghost of Steve Prefontaine and what the essence of running should be truly about.

I've been running—truly running—ever since, not for bumper decals or free T-Shirts, but for the sheer joy of it. To this day the only race I've ever run in my life was a mile fun run when I was ten, which ended in disaster. I ran out of gas trying to keep pace with the bigger boys and in the end, Jesse passed me with a quarter mile left to go, hunched over crying on the side of the trail with a cramp in my side. I ran that race for the wrong reasons, but I used the memory to serve as the foundation for what Fred was teaching me.

Steve Prefontaine was one of Fred's idols. For the uninitiated, he is considered by running enthusiasts to be the foremost expert on what running should be all about. It is a time to cleanse one's soul and thoughts and to find peace with whatever might be troubling you that particular day. Prefontaine once said, "A man can fail many times, but he isn't a failure until he begins to blame someone else." I think this was the message that resonated with Fred, and that which he was ultimately trying to pass on to me.

I am grateful for the lessons I've learned on my many runs over the last twenty years.

I run a lot. I don't care about the exact mileage. I've lost track anyway. I will never run another race, though I always get the same strange look when I try to explain my reasoning to others. Eventually I gave up trying to explain it. I'm not sure if they understand, nor is that important to me. I will continue to run for as long and hard as my mind and body will allow.

Fred used running as an analogy to teach me about the spiritual benefits of a healthy mind and body. Twenty years later, I still lean on him whenever I find myself needing clarity. I would not have the appreciation for life that I do if not for Fred Smith. He is my shaman.

JEDI BARISTA

After Fred was transferred, the idea of being an instructional assistant lost its luster rather quickly. If I was going to commit to the field of education, then I wanted to be a classroom teacher. I enjoyed working with students—I still do. It's the greatest gift of being an educator. But I felt intellectually unfulfilled in my role as an assistant. I hung on until the spring, supplementing my salary with additional student loans to cover my living expenses, then gave my two weeks' notice. I knew my life in education was not over; rather, it was just beginning. But I needed to work in the field on my own terms. My additional loans provided me with enough money to pay my bills for a month before hitting a financial pitfall.

At this point I was unemployed and taking night classes to complete my teaching certification. I would wake up, check the classifieds, study a little, and go to the beach. I was soon so broke that I worried I might be forced to move back to Cleveland, but I knew that I couldn't leave the beach to return to the wintry doldrums of the Midwest. I desperately needed a new routine. To keep myself occupied and on task, I decided to dedicate a few hours every morning to my studies before resuming the job hunt. However, since it doesn't take more than a paper bag to distract me if I'm alone and bored, studying in my apartment was out of the question.

I discovered a small mom-and-pop coffee shop in the historic downtown district that was perfect for my needs: the background noise and strong brew allowed me to focus, and I could take smoke breaks and people watch when I needed to get out of my head for a few minutes. A few days after I started going, I struck up a conversation with an older gentleman named Bill who, it transpired, was the proprietor of the establishment. The conversation was a casual one, mainly centered on my studies. He told me that his wife had been a teacher for over ten years, before quitting to help him open the coffee shop. They'd been in operation for over a decade now. I told him of my experiences as an instructional assistant and how I was currently out of work.

He chuckled to himself and asked me if I wanted to come work for him full time. Initially I thought it was a ruse, but I quickly realized he was serious. That was it. No interview or background check, we just shook hands and I told him I would see him early the next morning. Thus began my illustrious career as a barista.

Reminiscing some fifteen years later, it might have been the best job I ever worked. Bill owned two coffee shops, one near the beach and the other on Main Street in downtown Wilmington. I trained at the shop by the beach, which was actually a converted house with a drive thru. It was in this house that I became a Jedi of the coffee culture. The amazing assortment and quality of the beans filled the shop with a truly majestic aroma. Sometimes I would lift the lids of the five-gallon glass jars and just inhale as much as my lungs could manage. The coffee culture was all new to me. Until this point, my coffee had always come from whatever gas station I happened to pass in the mornings. I was eager to learn the intricate details that went into the business.

Over the first few days, Bill taught me the components necessary to run and maintain a coffee house. I learned how to work the register, which settings to use to grind the beans, what roasts brewed best at which temperatures, and all the alchemical accoutrements of the espresso bar. The sheer variety of espresso drinks that customers crave left my head spinning long after my shifts were over. I leaned heavily on Bill's tutelage and guidance. Most intriguing was not Bill's knowledge of coffee, but his interactions with the customers. We had a steady line at the register from six until eleven every morning; daily grinders sitting in their vehicles waiting to pull up and receive their fix. Bill instructed me to learn their faces, cars, drinks, and stories. My ability to memorize by rote came in handy again. The more I interacted with the customers, the better my bottom line was going to be.

By the end of the first week, I had customer's drinks waiting for them a car in advance. As I grew more comfortable with the coffee end of the business, I let my people skills fly in quick-hitting conversations, then on to the next customer. It was enough time to get their daily scoop, offer a word of encouragement, listen to them vent or, if I was lucky, get a little flirting in.

I could work a morning shift and end up with fifty dollars in tips. That was over two hundred dollars straight cash a week, plus the ten bucks an hour that Bill paid me. I banked my paychecks and lived off my tips during the week. My work schedule ran from five in the morning until noon, Monday through Friday. I dedicated my afternoons to my studies and some necessary beach time. After completing my training, I was moved to the downtown store to manage the morning crowd of the historic district. Working downtown was like nothing I had ever experienced before, and I was in awe. Being surrounded by so many people from so many walks of life, all against the quaint backdrop of the classic architecture along the Cape Fear River Port, opened my mind to the true beauty of humanity.

The downtown coffee shop was a one-person operation. Dawn was my domain, shared only with the occasional street sweeper with whom I would share a nod as I unlocked the old green door at five sharp every morning. I had a half hour to get the shop up and running before my first customers started trickling in at five-thirty. My morning regulars arrived like clockwork and never varied in their orders. When the church bells bonged out the six o'clock hour, I would step out onto the front stoop with a piping hot cup of fresh brew for a morning smoke. I would fire up a Lucky Strike and for five minutes, the world, though desolate, took on an eerie sense of peace.

The inside of the Main Street coffee shop was positively vintage. Along the left wall there were three long wooden shelves filled with five-gallon jars of coffee beans, off-staged and decorated with various antiques that Bill had collected over the years. The rustic hardwood floors and wooden tables complemented the two bay windows that looked out onto the street, and a pair of green rocking chairs sat to either side of the old glass-framed door. Walking inside was like stepping back into a simpler time.

It was an ideal spot for people watching, and provided me with a lot of contacts in the downtown community. I met a few well-known actors from the sitcom Dawson's Creek, a few of whom went on to have fairly successful careers in the movie industry. Some A-list actors occasionally made an appearance as well, as quite a few movies were filmed along Cape Fear during my years there. To me, they were just regular people that put their pants on one leg at a time. They didn't want to be drooled over while getting their morning coffee. They wanted their drink and a quick, friendly chat with a barista, and that is what I offered them. Unfortunately, all hope of invisibility vanished the moment they stepped out onto Main Street. Frankly, I got more excitement from seeing the local bartenders at the watering holes I frequented. I knew judges and lawyers that worked at the courthouse by their first name. I began to feel like an integral member of the community.

I lived six blocks from the river in a townhouse that I shared with one of Fred Smith's friends. An accomplished long-boarder and violin player, Shaku was a few years older than me and caught more damn waves in a session than anyone else on the beach. He rode with an unparalleled old school finesse.

We enjoyed meandering the six blocks to our favorite bars at twilight.

As I advanced further along in my academic studies, I began taking classes full-time at the university to complete my teacher certification, and my dawn shifts at the coffee shop grew less frequent, replaced by the evening shift. It was a different vibe, not nearly as many customers, but it still offered a feeling of mystique and ambiance that was as unique as the shop itself. There was still something magical about closing down for the evening and locking that old green door as the street lights were turning on. Some evenings, I would walk the six blocks to and from work just to take in the culture of that tiny port city. I enjoyed the vibe of the shop so much that I introduced Bill to Fred Smith.

Fred Smith and his family were moving to Oregon later that year, so he couldn't commit to another calendar year in the classroom. Bill liked Fred so much, he made him the manager of both shops. Fred worked my schedule around my academics. If I was busy, I didn't work. If I needed an extra shift, Fred took care of it. Fred was a people-person and took to the gig like he had never worked anywhere else in his life. It was a surreal time that lasted for almost a year. Eventually, Fred left for Oregon and I finished my teaching certification.

I took off for the summer, traveling to various National Parks around the country while living out of the back of my truck. When I returned home, it was time for me to complete my student teaching experience. I never went back to work at the coffee shop, but I will forever be grateful for the experience, and the chance that Bill took on me.

A WALK ON THE WATER

Within a few weeks of moving to Wilmington, I found myself drawn to the beach every day for sunset walks. After all the uncertainty in my life over the past few years, I was determined to make each day count. Every evening found me out there, hot or cold, rain or shine, and each walk along the crashing waves brought new revelations. I would certainly not advise walking a beach in a thunderstorm, but what an experience, to feel firsthand your own insignificance beside the power of the ocean.

It was during one of these evening strolls, as I watched a few graceful long-boarders in action, that I was overcome by the sudden, imperative desire to learn how to surf. Something about the act seemed so peaceful and spiritual in that moment, I knew I had to try.

I had been terrified of the ocean since the first time I watched Jaws. I was convinced growing up that an invisible twenty-foot shark lived in our backyard swimming pool and panicked every time I climbed the ladder because I thought it was going to bite me in the ass and drag me down to a watery death. I wasn't naive to the dangers of the Atlantic Ocean. I had heard stories from the prop pilots who flew banner advertisements over Wrightsville Beach of the many sharks they had seen from the air, skimming the surface of the ocean. I knew the risk here was substantially greater than the swimming in my backyard pool.

It took a great deal of internal coaxing to convince myself that I'd be alright. I'd go down to the beach and watch the

surfers paddle in and out of the line-up. They were only interested in catching waves, while I was on the lookout for dorsal
fins. One particular evening, I sat on the south end and counted
the thirty surfers that entered and exited the water without
incident. Finally, I made up my mind and overcame my fears
enough to venture into the surf shop a few miles from my apartment one evening after work. As I stood there overwhelmed
by the sheer variety of boards, new and used, that there were
to choose from, I happened to glance at a couple of price tags
and felt my eyebrows hit my hairline. In the back of my mind,
it occurred to me that this is how young people get themselves
into trouble with credit cards. After I came to grips with the
cost of my prospective hobby, I realized that I had no idea what
to look for in a surfboard. I was going to need some assistance
with the process of choosing the right board for me.

So there I stood, credit card in hand, spewing my Johnny
Utah story to the sun-bleached gentleman at the register, who
had probably heard the same nonsensical story ten times that
week. Nonetheless, he stood there chewing his nail and nodded
along, and though I'm sure he spent the whole interaction
thinking 'great, another idiot who's watched Point Break one
too many times,' he helped me pick out a used seven-foot-six
WRV (Wave Riding Vehicle) with a pointed nose that could
have speared Moby Dick. She was by no means the best board
in the shop, but she was the one I could afford, and he assured
me that if I worked on my technique I'd be catching waves with
her soon enough. I have never in my life felt sexier than when I
strapped that baby down in the back of my truck.

Besides the fact that I had no earthly idea how to surf, I had
one major strike against me in my quest to find the ultimate
ride: I had zero friends who surfed. Shaku and I were not to
link up until a year after I had begun my surfing pilgrimage,
so the only friend I had in town at that point was Fred Smith,
and his Irish ass was perfectly content to remain planted on dry

land. But surfing in solitude can be a beautiful adventure, as I eventually learned over the years. On the other hand, drowning or being eaten alive by a shark in isolation—not so enjoyable. But either way, actually knowing how to surf is an essential part of the process. In two decades of surfing, I would venture that I have surfed solo probably ninety-five percent of the time. I learned the craft by watching others surf in conditions that I would never paddle out into, observations that told me where to sit, when to paddle, and what position to get my board into for an approaching wave. Attempting to replicate what I watched was an entirely different scenario.

There is a trend in surfing culture that I was not aware of until I started paddling out: most surfers do not want to be in a lineup anywhere near someone who is trying to learn how to surf. Especially when the waves are the right condition. Wrightsville Beach gets some decent surf, but mostly it stays in the knee-to-thigh-high wave range. However, if the surf is clean, it can be a beautiful time, and experienced surfers are not interested in having anyone ruin their session. Yep, I was that guy for a while. No one tried to punch me out, but I did catch some really hard stares and even a few choice words on occasion. I just had to remind myself that none of these fellas were on the pro surfing circuit, and even if they were, they were surrounded by amateurs anyway, so what did it matter?

I learned rather quickly to surf off to the side, staying away from the pack. The waves didn't break as well out there, but I wasn't catching them anyways. I almost drowned a handful of times that first week trying to duck-dive my tank of a board under the crashing surf, which never worked too well. My board was too wide and long to push underneath the breaking waves. Finally, some older long-boarder took pity on me and taught me how to roll my board when I was about to get pounded. I was so exhausted from trying to get out past the breaking waves that often I would just lie on my board for fifteen minutes catching my breath. I thought I was in pretty decent shape, but I was definitely not in surfing condition, especially in my lungs.

Enjoying a mid-morning session at the south end of Wrightsville Beach.

Once I was consistently able to get past the breaking surf, my fear of sharks was the next major hurdle. I spent an eternity just floating around alone on my board. The ocean is abundant with gigantic fish, and I prayed to God constantly that I wouldn't be attacked. Funny enough, the thing that got to me the most wasn't the prospect of being eaten alive, but imagining the other surfers being interviewed by the local news crew and spending the whole segment talking about what a shit surfer I was. Numerous times, my fears got the best of me and I angled my board for shore and paddled with all my might, waiting at any second to be dragged to the depths below. I'd drive home pissed off at my lack of success given the amount of time I was spending, but the hope of one day standing up on my board always brought me back. I surfed even when there was no surf. I spent those nights working on my paddling technique while attempting to ride the occasional shore break.

Fortunately, for all my inexperience in the ocean, I could at least say that I was a strong swimmer. I grew up taking swim lessons at the community pool every summer, so I knew my strokes and breathing techniques. For Christ's sake, we had a pool from the time I was nine until my senior year of high school. We spent our summers swimming, even when my parents weren't home, which was strictly forbidden. I had spent years swimming in ponds, rivers, lakes, and even the mighty Erie. Yet, outside of my brother holding me under a little too long on occasion, I always knew the water wasn't going to take me hostage. However, all that changed a few months into my new endeavor.

The first time a wave really bucked me I thought nothing of it, until the leash that was attached to my ankle reached its maximum length, sending my surfboard flying overhead. The board and leash tossed effortlessly through the surf while I was dragged in the undertow, spastically and arduously attempting to surface. I swam down when I thought I was swimming up. My lungs were going to burst. For a moment, I even forgot to be afraid of sharks. I remember finally planting me feet firmly on the ocean floor and exploding toward the surface with all my might. I had just enough time to gasp for life before another wave sucked me back under. I was caught on the inside of a pounding surf.

It was past Labor Day, so there was no hope of a lifeguard being on hand, and it was unlikely that any of my fellow surfers would notice my plight as I did my best to keep out of their way. My only option was to claw for air and pray I made it out of this alive. I surfaced a second time amidst the whitewash of the breaking waves and was able to grab hold of my board. Too weak to pull myself onto it, I merely clung to it and let it drag me to shore like a shipwrecked sailor clinging to a piece of splintered lumber. When I was relatively close to the shore, I planted my feet in the shallow water and realized that I was shaking uncontrollably from the fading panic. Fear and exhaustion caused me to collapse in the wet sand while tears of terror, frustration, and failure surfaced. I sat there in amazement. No one had even witnessed the event. If I had not made it, only God knows if and when I would have been discovered. I pointed a finger to the sky and offered a prayer of thanks.

I thought my near-death experience would soften my desire to surf, but it didn't. I was back at it the next night, in slightly calmer waters and with a newfound respect for the sea. I learned to monitor the waves a little more closely, and to choose days with more ideal conditions.

Fortunately, those swells didn't really interest too many of the more experienced surfers in the area. As I improved my sense of balance, paddling out past the break became routine and I was able to maintain a seated position on my board. Facing the horizon, I was often overwhelmed by the sheer poetry of my surroundings, watching as the waves rolled in against the sunset. On those nights, I was more content to sit out on my board and watch the Atlantic in all its beauty. It was on that board that I found the spirituality that I had never really found in a chapel. On the water, I was at peace with myself and the world.

I continued to make that trek to the beach, even when the waves were flat and I was the only person sitting out on a surfboard. For a boy from Cleveland, the experience was so much more. I kept paddling, falling, and occasionally nearly drowning, though never to the degree of that particularly hellish day. One evening, I paddled my ass off and actually, finally, stood up on my board. The whitewater ride lasted for about three seconds, but I had broken through the final roadblock that had eluded me for what felt like an eternity. I stayed out that evening, well into twilight, riding wave after wave of whitewater. I still had no concept of the line of a wave or the graceful motion of traveling at an angle down its face. I wasn't there yet. I didn't care. I felt like a king as I tucked my board under my arm and made the walk across the beach toward my truck.

The better part of the next year was a surfing crusade that

taught me more about myself than I could have imagined. I experienced what it was like to surf the face of the wave. I learned that I was "goofy footed," meaning I prefer to go left on a breaking wave instead of right, but I began to take what the wave offered and appreciate it. My confidence grew to the point that I no longer avoided those packs of local boys that congested every decent break on the beach. Instead, I paddled out among them and fought like hell for the right to each wave.

But surfing with others soon taught me that I actually preferred to surf alone, and after battling for a few good waves I would head back to the outskirts. I found that for me, surfing was a meditative experience, very similar to running.

A SUMMER AGO

The time kept rolling with the tide, filling in the details of my life with each passing year. I met Stephanie, my wife, while completing my student teaching. She was a long-term substitute looking for her first permanent teaching position. The following year the local school hired us both back. Well, they hired me first and Steph shortly afterward, which led to a frigid period of several months before time would soften my Italian spitfire. We spent another year in Carolina before moving to Las Vegas, Nevada to teach for five years. Vegas was an experience worthy of its own memoir. But we knew we would return to Stephanie's childhood stomping grounds in northern Virginia after she became pregnant with our first son, Emmett.

We bought an old bungalow farm house in the country on a few acres, and spent a few years working on the house and land. Then came our Sawyer, the bean, and life got a little hectic with two young ones, teaching school, and a mini-farm. So we sold our land and our home to spend more time with our boys. I was finally freed up to coach my boy's baseball teams and take them on bike rides and to the community pool—all the things I had neglected for the past several years because I thought it was more important to fix an old house.

After we sold the bungalow, we moved into an old house that previously belonged to a family friend of ours. Elma was a pillar of the town of Herndon, a well-known artist and long-time secretary at both the local elementary and high schools. She passed away recently at the venerable age of ninety-three, leaving her lovely little place on Monroe Street empty. The place was built in 1904 on a foundation of stone and it couldn't be more perfect. At night, I sit on the massive paint-chipped porch listening to the rain ping and dance off the tin roof. The hardwood floors, wood cut-outs, and French doors remind me of a simpler time long forgotten. My boys share Elma's old bedroom, drifting off to sleep to the sound of my fingers striking the keyboard in the next room. Nightly, I walk out onto the second-story balcony to breathe, glancing at the new homes built around this classic old house. The second-story hardwood moans as I make my way down the hall after tucking my boys in for the night.

Last summer, I brought my family back to the south end of Wrightsville Beach for a vacation. Steph stayed back at the rental house, sipping coffee on the front porch just a few doors down from where I used to live. The boys and I tromped over to the beach early, with our boards and beach toys. We set up shop back on the dunes, near lifeguard tower number twelve, so the encroaching tide wouldn't wash away my boys' masterpieces. The Atlantic was a sheet of glass, with gentle thigh-high sets of waves rolling in. I was pleased to see that life here hadn't changed much since I last called this beach home.

"Dad, go surf," Emmett publicized loud enough for his younger brother to hear.

"Papa, I want to watch you ride the waves," Sawyer chimed in. Apprehensively, I paused, knowing Steph would be here shortly. I nodded in agreement as I watched my boys with sand shovels in hand etch out the foundation of their new sandcastle. I grabbed my board and started for the water. As I paddled into the break, I turned my head to see Steph making her way onto the beach toward our boys. A sense of peace came over me as I sat upright on my board to watch the waves. I missed the smell of the salty air, the taste of it on my lips, and the clarity of the blue water.

The memories of this place came flooding back to me. This

was where I learned to surf, began my career as an educator, came to peace with my past, and fell in love with the woman who became my wife. I traveled a long way back to get to this point, so I took a moment to reflect. Patiently waiting for my wave, I looked back at the beach again to check on my family. Steph and the boys stood in the shore break, shovels in hand, watching and waiting for their pops to walk on water. I was lost in my thoughts again. This beach and the ocean always did that to me. It didn't feel like twelve years had passed since the last time I paddled out at the south end. Time passed by so swiftly, yet there I was again, caught in the moment.

It was important to us that our boys had the opportunity to visit this place. They needed to see the houses we lived in, the places we worked, the restaurants and bars we frequented. This is essentially where it all began for them. Later that evening, I walked along the shoreline with Steph and the boys, looking for seashells like I did so many years ago with their mother. I held my wife's hand and reveled in the nostalgia of falling in love with her during our walks on this very beach. I'm glad we finally made it back there.

EPILOGUE

Twenty years have passed since I taught myself to surf. Another sip of coffee, and I am reminded with a jolt of the obligations waiting for me a few miles away. I told my wife and boys I needed to get a little gas in my tank, but that was over an hour ago and still no one has called to check in on me. Shocked, I am not. Stephanie knows me better than any other person in this world, maybe even myself. She recognizes when I am lost, fighting to find my way back, even if all I'm doing is sitting at the kitchen table staring into space. She has been there for me so many times when I couldn't be there for myself. For a fortnight of years, she has endured a roller-coaster ride of heartache and broken promises with the unwavering love of an angel. I always say that she punched her ticket to heaven the day we met.

I feel a sense of overwhelming peace as I pull the last drops from the bottom of the container. Maybe it's the caffeine? As the sun sets lower on the horizon, the ball field is cast in shadows and I realize that time is slipping away into evening. I best be heading on home. I know Stephanie and my boys will be waiting for me.

I'm right where I'm supposed to be. It just took me a minute to realize it.

Steph, Sawyer, and Emmett basking in the glory of our annual autumn apple picking tradition.

About the Author

Greg Drost grew up the middle child of three boys on the outskirts of Cleveland, Ohio. For the past seventeen years, he has been an elementary school teacher in North Carolina, Nevada, and Virginia. He currently resides in Northern Virginia with his wife and two sons.

CPSIA information can be obtained
at www.ICGtesting.com
Printed in the USA
BVHW030146220719
554042BV00001B/116/P